D0397695

A FIELD GUIDE TO

⟜« **INTERNET** »⟝

BOYFRIENDS

MEME-WORTHY CELEBRITY CRUSHES FROM A TO Z

»♡«

ESTHER ZUCKERMAN

ILLUSTRATIONS BY LOUISA CANNELL

RUNNING PRESS
PHILADELPHIA

Running Press
Hachette Book Group
1290 Avenue of the Americas, New York, NY 10104
www.runningpress.com
@Running_Press

Printed in China

First Edition: November 2020

Published by Running Press, an imprint of Perseus Books, LLC, a subsidiary of Hachette Book Group, Inc. The Running Press name and logo is a trademark of the Hachette Book Group.

The Hachette Speakers Bureau provides a wide range of authors for speaking events. To find out more, go to www.hachettespeakersbureau.com or call (866) 376-6591.

The publisher is not responsible for websites (or their content) that are not owned by the publisher.

Print book cover and interior design by Jenna McBride.

Library of Congress Control Number: 2020940024

ISBNs: 978-0-7624-7199-7 (hardcover), 978-0-7624-7200-0 (e-book)

RRD-S

10 9 8 7 6 5 4 3 2 1

CONTENTS

INTRODUCTION

Celebrity crushes are nothing new. For almost as long as there have been famous people, we plebeians have gazed upon their beautiful visages and imagined what it would be like to be in their company. I mean, when you look at it a certain way, even *The Aeneid* was sort of fan fiction, as were many of Shakespeare's plays. The early days of Hollywood had *Photoplay* magazine. From the '60s through the 2000s, teen fans could pin spreads from *Tiger Beat* on their walls. More mature readers had *People*'s Sexiest Man Alive starting in the mid-1980s. Now, there's the internet.

The internet has drastically changed the way we, as a collective public, interact with celebrities. There are still paparazzi pics and revealing interviews with artfully posed glamour shots, but social media has offered stars a direct line to our hearts. And it's not just about what a person posts—though demeanor online can garner great affection if done correctly. But these days fans also have control over their favorite's cultural presence. Through Tumblr, Twitter, and the like we have the power to isolate exactly what we find so appealing about an actor or musician or athlete or even politician and elevate them to new heights. We can create supercuts of their most charming moments. We can write long yarns imagining their activities. In other words, we can stan for days.

And thus Internet Boyfriends were born. The first person commonly regarded to have been deemed the "internet's boyfriend" was Benedict Cumberbatch, the British actor with the officious demeanor and confounding face who instigated Cumbermania around the year 2013. But there were other early Internet Boyfriends. Cumberbatch's fellow Brits Tom Hiddleston and Idris Elba won the title, as did Ryan Gosling, who became a receptacle for all our visions of an ideal man. Over the years Internet Boyfriends have come and gone. Rami Malek was one for a while, but turned into something of an Internet Villain instead during his Oscar run for *Bohemian Rhapsody*. Even Cumberbatch has arguably fallen out of favor.

What makes someone an Internet Boyfriend (or Girlfriend)? As with anything that was created by a hive mind, it's an amorphous concept that means different things to different people. The simplest definition of an Internet Boyfriend is someone who people on the internet love. But that doesn't quite capture it. (A lot of people on the internet love Donald Trump, for instance.) To refine, an Internet Boyfriend is someone who gets almost entirely good press, who either gives zero fucks or just the right number of fucks, who seems like the type of person you would probably want to get to know and definitely want to date. An Internet Boyfriend often plays characters that are just as intriguing—or even more intriguing—than the Internet Boyfriend himself. An Internet Boyfriend *represents* something.

Writing in 2016, in a piece for *New York Magazine*'s The Cut entitled "How the Internet Picks Its Boyfriends," Sulagna Misra defined these men as such: "When real men disappoint us—in their politics, their bullshit, their basic human inconsistencies—the internet's boyfriend is a paragon of enlightened masculinity, constructed by committee." The term has evolved and mutated even since Misra wrote her nearly definitive piece, but this remains essential to the notion of an Internet Boyfriend: "Usually it's someone surrounded by an aura of authenticity. There must be a conception (whether it's true is moot) that he earned his current position through hard work rather than dumb luck."

Writers since Misra have tried to argue for further specificity of the Internet Boyfriend. In *Cosmopolitan* in 2018, Emily Tannenbaum made the case that there was a distinction between Internet Boyfriends, the younger generation, and Internet Husbands, the older. "An Internet Boyfriend is the sexy new fling you want to show off (and maybe get naked with)," she wrote. "An Internet Husband is someone you want to cuddle, who makes you feel safe . . . and you still want to get naked with." Others might counter that by saying there doesn't necessarily need to be anything sexual about an Internet Boyfriend. But, maybe, just maybe, there does.

The very nature of the internet has made it easier than ever to publicly declare your love for a celebrity. This generation's cultural critics grew up knowing that there was no shame in being one of the kids screaming on the tarmac when the Beatles arrived in America in 1964 or outside the Virgin Megastore waiting for *NSYNC in 2000. They channeled their affections creatively. Who chooses Internet Boyfriends and Girlfriends? Largely women and queer people. This is not a straight man's game, though he can participate if he stays in line and doesn't make things weird. Online lust can get playfully objectifying, but should never be exploitative or alienating—or, frankly, sexist.

Meanwhile, writers have developed a way of turning their devotion to specific stars into clever content. The dearly departed website The Toast had a recurring column "If X Were Your Y," which began in 2015. The variables were always at liberty to shift, but the most common hypothetical was "If [Celebrity] Were Your [Boyfriend/Girlfriend]." Channing Tatum was the inaugural entry. Writers Bim Adewunmi and Nichole Perkins launched their podcast Thirst Aid Kit in 2017, which is both unapologetically horny and thoughtful as the hosts spend each episode fawning over and reading fan fiction about men, many of whom could be deemed Internet Boyfriends. The Cut meanwhile has a series in which they wonder whether a certain celebrity usually not thought of as "totally kind of hot" is actually "totally kind of hot," like Bill Hader or Marc Maron. But for as much as we've learned to embrace our desires, we've also become wary as of late. The #MeToo movement has put us on alert, ready to sniff out false prophets, men whose perceived goodness is just an act.

In this book, I will introduce you to a wide array of Internet Boyfriends and Girlfriends and attempt to explain just how they achieved that moniker. Again, you can try to track an Internet Boyfriend's or Girlfriend's ascension all you want, but there is always going to be something subjective about fandom. Behavior that's cute to one person is off-putting to another. You just might not "get" someone in this book, and that's fine. The people featured aren't perfect. They make mistakes. Some have had very public scandals. But they are mostly a net good in our society. Looking at them all collected together hopefully paints a picture of what plugged-in people have gravitated toward in this day and age. What is certain is that these people are not homogenous. An Internet Boyfriend is not one thing, but to the people that love him, he's everything.

A GLOSSARY OF IMPORTANT
INTERNET BOYFRIEND AND
GIRLFRIEND TERMINOLOGY

BAE:

The term, like many on the internet, is originally attributed to Black culture, but was co-opted by just about everyone— including corporations. It's a significant other, like, well, a boyfriend.

BDE:

Big dick energy. Coined by Kyrell Grant. According to Grant: "BDE has less to do with confidence and more to do with personality and how you carry yourself. And you don't need a dick to have it." BDE is swag. It's a mindset. You don't have to be big, in any way, to have big dick energy. Noted havers of BDE: Pete Davidson, Cate Blanchett, Beyoncé.

DADDY:

Colloquially thought of as a middle-aged to older gentleman with sex appeal. For instance, David Harbour on *Stranger Things* is "daddy." But, also, a daddy does not have to be older. It's complicated.

INTERNET GIRLFRIEND:

An Internet Boyfriend, but a woman.

MEME:

You know what a meme is! That's why we're here. Technically, a meme, according to Merriam-Webster is, "an idea, behavior, style, or usage that spreads from person to person within a culture." But you and I both know that's just the broadest possible definition. Memes are when the internet takes something and runs with it. They are white block text over a funny image. They are a tweet featuring Baby Yoda. They are Rihanna, in a gown, looking like a pizza. Memes generate Internet Boyfriends, and Internet Boyfriends generate memes. Memes are how we live.

OTP:

"one true pairing." A couple that shippers really want to be together. See: *Shipping*.

SHIPPING:

To ship—as in "relationship"—is to want fictional characters to be together, romantically. Some people ship Captain America and Bucky Barnes.

SLASH FICTION:

Slash fiction is an outgrowth of fan fiction. However, these stories about preexisting characters are really horny. Slash fiction is about sex—sex between two male characters who may or may not be gay in the source material.

SOFT BOY OR SOFTBOY:

A sweetie pie. Someone who gives the impression of being vulnerable. BuzzFeed once described him as "nonthreatening, nontoxic, and knows how to wear a pastel."

STAN:

Derived from the 2000 Eminem song of the same name, a stan is a really serious fan of someone. It can be used as a noun or a verb. For example, "I am a Lady Gaga stan" or "We stan a legend."

STEP ON MY NECK:

It's sort of inexplicable, but it's what we sometimes want our favorite celebrities to do to us. Young stans started asking their faves to obliterate them on Twitter, in a trend noticed by The Cut's Gabriella Paiella. She argued: "The joke's popularity may also have to do with the fact that we're living during a time when we're constantly being reminded that the Earth is going to be virtually uninhabitable by the end of the century, that capitalism is wholly unsustainable, and that we're just one push of a button away from perishing in a nuclear war." See also: "run me over with a car, daddy."

THIRST:

In other words, lust. When you look at a person and just get parched because they are so freaking hot. As a term, *thirst* was first used in the Black community, and sometimes can have a derogatory connotation. If you're posting too many selfies in an effort to get likes, that can be thirsty too.

VIRAL:

We're not talking about a disease! We're talking about an internet sensation spreading like proverbial wildfire across our feeds!

ZADDY:

Zaddies are hard to define. Most broadly they are really sexually magnetic guys, often, but not always, of a certain age. Clover Hope wrote in Jezebel that: "Immediately, you know in your heart who's not a zaddy. It's an instinctual response that's not worth explaining in depth because you're supposed to just feel it." Zaddies are sort of like porn, as defined by the Supreme Court: You know them when you see them.

WHICH INTERNET BOYFRIEND
IS RIGHT FOR YOU?

In this book you'll meet a variety of Internet Boyfriends. Old Internet Boyfriends. Young Internet Boyfriends. Musician Internet Boyfriends. But which one is right for you? Take this handy quiz and find out.

YOUR IDEAL DAY INVOLVES?	**A.** A lengthy gym session, bro **B.** A motorcycle ride **C.** A beach trip **D.** A rooftop chill session with some acoustic guitar **E.** A shopping spree

DRINK OF CHOICE?	**A.** A light beer **B.** A finely aged Pinot Noir **C.** A rum cocktail **D.** A craft beer **E.** No drink, just some 'shrooms

FAVORITE SCORSESE MOVIE?	**A.** *The Departed* **B.** *After Hours* **C.** *Goodfellas* **D.** *Alice Doesn't Live Here Anymore* **E.** *The Aviator* (You covet Katharine Hepburn's trousers.)

FAVORITE TAYLOR SWIFT ALBUM?	**A.** *Taylor Swift* **B.** *Reputation* **C.** *Fearless* **D.** *Red* **E.** *1989*

FAVORITE BEYONCÉ ALBUM?	**A.** *B'Day* **B.** *Homecoming: The Live Album* **C.** *Beyoncé* **D.** *Lemonade* **E.** *4*

WHERE WOULD YOU MOST LIKE TO LIVE?	**A.** Boston **B.** A secluded cabin where no one can find you **C.** Los Angeles **D.** New York **E.** A flat in Notting Hill

YOU WOULD DESCRIBE YOURSELF AS?	**A.** Traditional 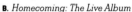 **B.** Mysterious **C.** Fun **D.** Creative **E.** A little kooky

FAVORITE AUTHOR?	**A.** Herman Melville **B.** Franz Kafka **C.** Haruki Murakami **D.** Shakespeare **E.** Jane Austen

YOU ANSWERED:

MOSTLY As

A Chris! Any Chris! Pick a Chris! You are a little bit basic but you have a good heart.

MOSTLY Bs

Keanu Reeves. You are mysterious and have an adventurous side. You like things that challenge you. You are often misunderstood.

MOSTLY Cs

Michael B. Jordan. You are a classic. You are overflowing with style and you love a good time.

MOSTLY Ds

Oscar Isaac. You are very artistic, but you like to keep things down-to-earth.

MOSTLY Es

Harry Styles. You're a bit funky. You want to experiment. You are trying to leave your past behind, but also have an affection for history.

♥

THE

INTERNET

BOYFRIENDS

♥

Now that you know what the terminology is and you have figured out which Internet Boyfriend is perfect for you, let's meet some of them. Here, arranged in alphabetical order, are the Internet Boyfriends and Girlfriends I have chosen to highlight. The selection process was admittedly difficult, and there will definitely be some of your beloveds who didn't make the cut. This is in part due to my personal taste, and in part due to a desire to showcase as wide a variety of Internet Boyfriends and Girlfriends as possible. (Sorry Tom Hardy fans. Please forgive me.)

You might even argue that some of these are not *precisely* Internet Boyfriends. Some are Internet Girlfriends. Some are Internet Zaddys. Some are Internet Best Friends. But for one reason or another we absolutely love them.

SEXY SUBJECT:

MAHERSHALA ALI

PLACE OF ORIGIN: Bay Area

NATURAL HABITAT: Los Angeles, but he looks amazing on any beach

ATTRIBUTES: Big smile, avant-garde sense of style, unparalleled acting chops

Mahershala Ali seems to exist in a perpetual state of coolness. And I don't just mean cool in that arbitrary sense that's impossible to define—though I sort of do. Everything he does is awe-inspiring—and he looks amazing while doing it.

Mahershala Ali accepting not one but two Oscars in a three-year time span is extremely cool. Ali accepting his first of those two Oscars in an all black ensemble, just days after he became a father, is cool. Ali, a proud Muslim man, receiving the highest award in his industry in the wake of Donald Trump's immigration ban, is cool. Ali accepting his second Oscar in what is essentially a "formal beanie" and big wire-framed glasses is also cool. Ali playing the part-vampire superhero Blade for the Marvel Cinematic Universe is *cool*. Very cool.

Besides that ineffable "coolness," Mahershala Ali comes off as coolheaded—intense, yes, but in a manner that is deliberate without seeming weirdly over-engineered, the way some celebrities can come off when speaking to the press. He's someone who thinks and speaks deeply about race and representation, who has become a leader in the Muslim American community, who gives performances that are soul deep. In his best work he radiates a sort of calm, like in *Moonlight* when he carefully takes a young boy's heartbreaking question about a gay slur and softly explains the cowardice of the people who wield that word.

But, for as cool as he is, Mahershala Ali also has a warmth about him. It's probably why he looks so damn good in warm tones. The women of the Thirst Aid Kit podcast say he "invented the color yellow," no doubt because of a *GQ* photo shoot in which he poses in various items all rendered in the primary tone. That wasn't the *GQ* spread of his that garnered the most attention, however. His cover story very well broke the internet. The headline at the African American news site Bossip says it all really: "The Thirst: Mahershala Ali Hasn't Left A Single Dry Panty On Twitter All Damn Day." Black Girl Nerds tweeted: "Going to look at more Mahershala Ali smiling photos for self care." *Harper's Bazaar* declared his smile "contagious."

The shoot captures Ali on Catalina Island in California, basking in the sun, his printed shirts various levels of unbuttoned as he basically frolics by the beach. It's pretty much the most joyful thing you've ever seen, as well as the most beautiful. But the meditative Ali is present as well. In the accompanying story by the author Carvell Wallace, Ali wrestles with identity and race.

Ali had been a working actor for a long time before he got the breaks that would make the internet take notice. The buzz started with his guest work on *House of Cards* as the lobbyist Remy Danton, then got more traction when he played the villainous Cottonmouth on another Netflix show, *Luke Cage*. But the turning point was *Moonlight*. In Barry Jenkins's film, which would ultimately—and very dramatically, given a mishap with the envelopes—win Best Picture, he played Juan, a drug dealer who becomes a father figure to the central character. Ali's turn is a tender deconstruction of how Black masculinity is usually depicted on-screen, culminating in a gorgeous scene set in Miami's ocean waters. Basically, as soon as the movie hit, he was labeled the Best Supporting Actor front-runner, and his life changed.

Then came the glamour shots, the Twitter screaming, and the accolades. Ali won the Oscar for *Moonlight*, the same weekend his wife, artist Amatus Sami-Karim, gave birth to their first child. On the campaign trail for the film, he spoke up about his own beliefs in light of Donald Trump's announcement of an immigration ban.

He'd win his next Oscar in two years' time for *Green Book*, a movie that was less beloved to say the least. It says something about Ali's power that the controversy surrounding that movie—and specifically its portrayal of the character he was playing—ended up not affecting his Internet Boyfriend status at all. When the film was taken to task for how it prioritized the story of the bigoted Italian guy (played by Viggo Mortensen) who learns to be less racist over that of the virtuosic Black pianist, Ali himself was not put through the court of think pieces. It's partially because what we adore about Ali is that he is not someone who seems to speak or act from the gut with no filter.

He also doesn't lean into his thirst trap status. In fact, it's very much the opposite. For as much as Twitter wants to declare him a god among men, he would rebuke that notion. Early in his career, as he explained to *Esquire*, he was even passing on roles that were divine in any way because of his devotion to Islam, which he converted to in 1999. He said: "I've mellowed out since. Now I think that for the purposes of art, I can play those roles as human beings, not gods. I can also differentiate between what I believe, and what the story's saying. But at the time, I was new, just figuring it out. I had no one to have that conversation with." He also doesn't take roles that would require him to have a sex scene. It's not that he plays characters who don't have sex, but he doesn't want to simulate it on-screen. Whatever he's doing, Mahershala Ali is not taking anything lightly.

Just because Ali isn't embracing his status as a thirst icon doesn't mean that he doesn't care about fashion or that his sense of fashion isn't one of the reasons he's achieved Internet Boyfriend status. But that too is considered. His sense of style is not for shock value alone. It's all part of a carefully considered plan to subvert expectations of men on red carpets. He partnered with Zegna on a line meant to interrogate the question: "What does it mean to be a man today?"

Which all leads us back to that coolness. The very word *cool* gets an often rightfully bad reputation. It doesn't really mean anything, but you look at Mahershala Ali and think: That is a cool person. He's cool because his style is something that feels fresh and new. He's cool because he has principles that he stands up for and espouses in his public persona. Just cool.

A FIELD GUIDE TO INTERNET BOYFRIENDS

SEXY SUBJECT:

TIMOTHÉE CHALAMET

PLACE OF ORIGIN: New York City

NATURAL HABITAT: Tompkins Square Bagels

ATTRIBUTES: Hypebeast aesthetic, angular features, floppy hair

One phenomenon in the world of Internet Boyfriends worth exploring is the soft boy. In a way, most Internet Boyfriends have a little soft boy to them. Soft boys project vulnerability in a way that makes them seem both admirable and approachable. They are sort of floppy in countenance—and sometimes a little squirrelly in body language. They seem unthreatening and ultimately kind. And if they have a king, it is Timothée Chalamet.

Where to begin with the man known colloquially as Timmy and—to those who are aware of his alter ego—Lil' Timmy Tim. Probably the best place to start is 2017, the year he emerged as the Next Big Thing and changed many a stan's life forever.

It all started with *Call Me By Your Name*. The Luca Guadagnino film, an adaptation of a novel by André Aciman, cast Chalamet as Elio Perlman, a teenager spending the summer at his parents' gorgeous Italian home who becomes smitten with a confident graduate student named Oliver, played by a larger than life (in every way) Armie Hammer. When *Call Me By Your Name* premiered at the Sundance Film Festival, it was immediately hailed as new queer classic. By the time it was about to hit theaters in November, Chalamet had become a phenomenon.

It's impossible to imagine that Chalamet would have risen to the level of fame and obsession he currently occupies without *Call Me By Your Name*. It's Elio that solidified his Internet Boyfriend status. Why? Because Elio himself is obsessed.

The reason why we all decided to love Timothée as Elio so much was because Timothée as Elio *is* us. Elio is an unbridled combination of awkwardness and horniness, just like basically everyone who spends a lot of time on the internet. He is infatuated by someone who seems unattainable, just like we are. His devotion leads him to get a little weird, like the moment when he sneaks into Oliver's room and smells his swimming shorts or when he gets, ahem, intimate with a peach. (Cue the emojis.) As a character Elio is unabashedly emotional, and Chalamet makes those emotions palpable. He is the human embodiment of having "the feels." Our collective fantasy of Timothée Chalamet is that he will just sit with us facing a fireplace while we both quietly sob to Sufjan Stevens like he does at the end of *Call Me By Your Name*.

Of course, his other breakout performance offers a counter to this. In Greta Gerwig's *Lady Bird*, released the same year as *CMBYN*, he's Kyle, a too-cool-for-school rich kid who reads Howard Zinn and offers the heroine played by Saoirse Ronan only the vaguest form of flirtation. He's an avatar for every douchebag we ever fell in love with in high school, who reads one social history of the United States and then decides that cell phones are bad and anarchy is good. Kyle is Oliver to

Lady Bird's Elio, but their quote-unquote passionate affair consists of a very disappointing sexual encounter.

It's just this *idea* of obsession that hovers around Chalamet and makes him somehow both relatable and the subject of other people's adoration. It's there in his performance in Gerwig's *Little Women* too. As Laurie, the March girls' neighbor, he's completely smitten with Louisa May Alcott's foursome and the creative lives they lead. Jo (Ronan, again) is the object of his affection, and when she spurns him, he ends up finding love with Florence Pugh's Amy. It's like he just needs to be accepted into these women's lives in any way possible. He plays Laurie like a kitten chasing after a string—adorable and needy.

But what about Timothée in real life? Yes, turns out it's a trend. Profiling him for Vulture, journalist Kyle Buchanan explored how big of a fanboy Chalamet is. Chalamet has been on the record about his love for Amar'e Stoudemire, Kid Cudi, and the Safdie brothers, gritty filmmakers from New York. He loves Greta Gerwig so much that he calls her "Wayne Gretzky." In interviews, he displays an unbridled enthusiasm for the stuff he likes that comes off as a tad dorky—gangly limbs flying all over the place, a low giggle punctuating his speech. The comedian Chloe Fineman does an impression of him that's exaggerated, but spot on: In her interpretation, he's unable to get through a sentence without issuing a deep laugh and clapping his hands together.

Watching Chalamet, you can't help but recall his own embarrassing adolescent moments, the ones that shape the Timothée legacy of doing a little too much, but in an endearing way. To be a Timmy fan is to know about his identity Lil' Timmy Tim and that time he rapped about statistics while he was a student at Fiorello H. LaGuardia High School of Music & Art and Performing Arts, aka the *Fame* school. Sure, he was a preternaturally talented kid, but at his heart he's just a goofball.

All documented interactions with Chalamet seem giddy. He brought bagels to the premiere of his Netflix movie *The King* because his frequent visits to Tompkins Square Bagels in New York have become part of his identity. He once interacted with his self-proclaimed biggest fan, a Twitter user named Derek, via FaceTime on another red carpet.

As Chalamet's star has grown, he's gotten a little more polished. He is now a budding style icon, showing up to events in outfits that mash up street style with androgyny. He'll wear a harness to the Oscars, and a sequined hoodie to the London Film Festival. When he's posing, he affects a model-esque smize, slightly pursing his lips to highlight his angular jawline. But when the cameras capture him in candid moments, he's got that big broad smile on his face and the illusion of the untouchable red-carpet staple falls away. It's back to the same old wide-eyed Timothée, king of the soft boys, who, in an ideal world, is just as happy to meet you as you are to meet him.

NOAH CENTINEO

If Timothée Chalamet is the Internet Boyfriend for the Gen Z art house set, Centineo is for the Netflix and Chill aficionados. He's a little goofier, a little buffer, and a little more mainstream. Chalamet is the theater kid smoking a cigarette underneath the bleachers while he reads up on Samuel Beckett. Centineo is the affable jock with a sensitive soul. He's slightly less refined, which doesn't make him any less of a big old hunk.

Of course, Noah Centineo would not be anything without Peter Kavinsky. He only achieved Internet Boyfriend status thanks to his role playing the ideal boyfriend in the Netflix original movie *To All the Boys I've Loved Before*, based on the Jenny Han book of the same name. Peter Kavinsky is every teen girl's fantasy wrapped up into one wide-grinned, curly-haired package.

The premise for those of you who somehow missed the phenomenon: Shy Lara Jean Covey (Lana Condor) writes elaborate notes to her crushes, which she then tucks away into a box, thus hiding her true feelings. One day, thanks to her nosy sister, all those letters get mailed, including the one addressed to Peter. Sure, sure, there's a whole elaborate love triangle, but to cut to the point Lara Jean and Peter start fake-dating. *That* ultimately turns into real dating because *OF COURSE THEY ARE MEANT TO BE TOGETHER.*

Centineo was known before *To All the Boys*. He was on the TV show *The Fosters* and the extremely popular Camila Cabello video "Havana." But no one had seen anything like Peter Kavinsky from him before. Peter Kavinsky is supersweet. He goes all the way across town to pick up the yogurt drinks Lara Jean likes at the Korean grocery store. Peter Kavinsky knows how to work his hands. Case in point, during the movie's crucial hot tub scene—yes, I said hot tub scene—he flicks the water just so.

When *To All the Boys* dropped in the summer of 2018, the reaction to Centineo was instant. He was the subject of glowing profiles like the one in *New York Magazine* in which he confessed: "I'm fucking so romantic. Like, such a romantic—it's not even funny. I can't help it. I swear to God, like, every day, the majority of my day is sentimental. You know, I'm thinking about past relationships I've been in, how I miss them so much or what I would do different, or why I wanna be with them again, or just moments I'd like to go back to or I know why I shouldn't go back, and then you know, it's just constantly love, love, love."

It's statements like that that only help Centineo's case. Instead of being standoffish about his affections—the way so many men are perceived to be—he's overwhelmingly, gushingly open about his desire for romance. He's also still, well, sort of a bro. He cites the shocking French filmmaker Gaspar Noé as one of his favorites, singling out Noé's movie *Love*, which opens with a shot of ejaculation.

Centineo followed up *To All the Boys* with two other Netflix rom-coms: *Sierra Burgess is a Loser* and *The Perfect Date*, establishing him as the 1990s Tom Hanks of direct-to-computer content. (But, you know, sort of hotter.) The ultimate question with Noah Centineo is whether his Internet Boyfriend status has staying power. What happens when he can't play the confident but understanding high school dreamboat anymore? Does he have the range? Will the internet fall out of love? Or is he destined to become this generation's Jonathan Taylor Thomas, blessed by nostalgia, but cursed to live forever in that past?

BENEDICT CUMBERBATCH

PLACE OF ORIGIN: London

NATURAL HABITAT: A period drama

ATTRIBUTES: Otter-like features, mispronunciation of the word *penguin*

The internet existed long before Benedict Cumberbatch came on the scene, but somehow the lavishly named British star with a confoundingly attractive face that also somehow looks like an errant limb became the proto-Internet Boyfriend. How? Tumblr, largely.

David Karp founded Tumblr in 2007 as a home for "microblogging." Sure, you *could* write lengthy posts on the platform, but you could also fill your page with GIFs and memes and "retumbles." It was an inherently visual medium, perfect for fandoms and thirst. And then *Sherlock* premiered.

Benedict Cumberbatch had roles before *Sherlock*, but none of those came even slightly close to the level of impact the series would eventually have. Creators Mark Gatiss and Steven Moffat reimagined Arthur Conan Doyle's prickly hero for the digital age. In the show, Sherlock's coat billows as he solves mysteries with his extraordinary mind that operates like a computer while his pal and partner Watson blogs about their exploits. Moffat and Gatiss envisioned Sherlock as social media celebrity, which was fitting because that's what they wrought.

If you've ever seen a picture of Benedict Cumberbatch, you know that Benedict Cumberbatch is no one's obvious idea of a sex symbol. His eyes and mouth are small. His face is both angular and somehow mushy-seeming. He has been compared to an otter on multiple occasions. Moffat has said that the BBC almost rejected casting him as Sherlock claiming he was not the "sexy" sleuth they were envisioning. Little did they know, there would soon be legions of fans armed with evidence to the contrary like the button-down that was labeled the "Purple Shirt of Sex," because, well, it was both fairly low cut and stirred all kinds of feelings.

Cumberbatch's trajectory is nothing unusual for a white British actor. He went to a fancy prep school and eventually landed at the London Academy of Music and Dramatic Art. Then he started doing Shakespeare on stage and getting notable but small parts in films like *Atonement*. (He plays a total creep in that one.)

It seems unlikely that the fandom around Cumberbatch would have ever exploded the way it did without *Sherlock*. The eponymous character is written as essentially asexual, and yet, Cumberbatch somehow injects sexual chemistry into every relationship, most notably into his partnership with Martin Freeman's Watson and antagonistic ballet with the villainous Moriarty, played by Andrew Scott. (Scott's Internet Boyfriend status would later be solidified when he played the "hot priest" on Internet Girlfriend Phoebe Waller-Bridge's *Fleabag* nearly ten years later.) It was slash fiction heaven.

Sherlock and Watson and Sherlock and Moriarty were *perfect* candidates for this particularly sexual brand of creative writing inspired by a preexisting property. As of writing, there are 5,000 pages of content dedicated to *Sherlock* on the hub Archive of Our Own. *Sherlock* fan fiction allowed people to turn subtext into text and make Cumberbatch's creation act out their fantasies however explicit.

If Sherlock was aloof and brimming with tension, Cumberbatch himself long ago proved to be sweet-seeming in person, as Jada Yuan noted in a profile for *New York Magazine* at the height of the Cumberbatch frenzy. He went on Graham Norton's BBC talk show and revealed his inability to say the word *penguin*, pronouncing it "*penwing.*" Footage of his motion capture performance in as the dragon Smaug in *The Hobbit* movies brimmed with theater kid enthusiasm. He taunted his eager fans by once responding to a Reddit question about whether he and other Internet Boyfriends like onetime *Doctor Who* star Matt Smith and Loki actor Tom Hiddleston polished their cheekbones: "We like nothing better than buffing our Zygoma. And imagining a horny time traveling long overcoat purple scarf wearing super sleuth nordic legend fuck fantasy. Get to work on that, internet." He entertained all the silly permutations of his name that emerged online. And, perhaps the crowning achievement, he thought his female fans were degrading themselves by assigning the "Cumberbitch" moniker to their identity.

Ah, yes, "Cumberbitch." Standom names are typically reserved for pop stars—see, for instance, the Beyhive and the Swifties—but Cumberbatch's cadre came up with a clever if crude way to define themselves. Just swap an "a" for an "i" and you've made something posh a little bit dirty. Cumberbatch himself was a little suspicious of "Cumberbitch," but for a reason that won him even more adoration: He worried it just wasn't quite feminist enough. Over the years he suggested "Cumber Collective" and "Cumberpeople"; Cumberbabes and Cumberbunnies also wormed their way into the lexicon. But his concern all just went to prove that he was exactly what his fans wanted him to be.

It's hard to pinpoint when the Cumberbatch mania started to wane or what caused it to quell. One argument for its demise is that he played the same version of a character one too many times and that type of man grew less appealing over time. In 2013, the cocky, overly self-assured genius was dominating screens big and small; by 2016, when Cumberbatch played the cocky, overly self-assured Doctor Strange in his very own Marvel movie, that kind of antihero had fallen out of fashion. In the years since, the internet has liked its boyfriends to be a little more vulnerable than Cumberbatch has ever appeared.

Even Tom Hiddleston, Cumberbatch's fellow Brit, who was dominating Tumblr around the same time he was, has a less chilly reputation despite still being best loved for playing the villain Loki.

And yet we can't overstate the influence of Cumberbatch and his Cumber-whatever-you-want-to-call-them. The posh Englishman with the funny name ushered in our current era of obsession. He is one of the patron saints of Internet Boyfriends.

RYAN GOSLING

If the history of modern Internet Boyfriends started in earnest with Benedict Cumberbatch
(see page 31), Ryan Gosling is
the Internet Boyfriend's pre-
history. He's the Neanderthal,
if you will—but in a really cute
way. The internet took and

modeled Ryan Gosling in its own image. His face became a
canvas on which to project all of its desires. Through no design
of his own, this man became a meme.

First, there was "Hey Girl," which began around 2008. It
was a simple format. A picture of Ryan Gosling along with a
superimposed caption in direct address. Sample: "Hey Girl, I
can't wait to meet your parents and all of your friends." Yes, as
Jezebel noted in 2009, it basically presupposes that Gosling is
your boyfriend. "Hey Girl" was just the beginning though.

The Feminist Ryan Gosling Tumblr—and subsequent book—
evolved "Hey Girl" into something more intellectual. The brain-
child of Danielle Henderson, a writer who at that point was in
school for gender studies, the blog used the same format as
"Hey Girl," but this time Gosling was spouting the teachings
of Betty Friedan and Simone de Beauvoir. In the introduction
to her book, Henderson explained that while Gosling, at the
time, had never actually indicated that he knew the work of,

say, Audre Lorde, using him as a mouthpiece made a certain amount of sense. "He is charming, talented, and intelligent; he has said some things in the media that can be construed as feminist. He loves his mom and takes ballet," she wrote.

If that was too high-minded for you, there was always the Vine sensation "Ryan Gosling Won't Eat His Cereal." Writer-director Ryan McHenry invented this format, in which he would hold out a spoonful of cereal to an on-screen Gosling who would appear to refuse the offering.

Gosling, of course, is a lovable movie star, but nothing he did really provoked this onslaught of attention. He didn't come out and say, "I am a feminist"—though he *has* said things that can be interpreted as feminist—or declare his hatred of breakfast foods. It was just that he seemed to serve as a spark of inspiration for a bunch of people around the start of the last decade.

Naturally, there were other, more obvious, reasons why he was a crush object. Gosling got his start on the Mickey Mouse Club with all the pop stars of the late '90s like Justin Timberlake and Britney Spears, but he was elevated to major crush status in 2004 when *The Notebook* came out. The Nicholas Sparks adaptation established him as *the* sex symbol of the early aughts, an excellent movie kisser, and the guy with whom you want to be stuck out on a boat in the rain. The moment he and Rachel McAdams won best kiss at the MTV Movie Awards for that movie just further cemented his place in our hearts. Wearing a shirt that just said "Darfur," he lifted her aloft, defining fantasies for years to come. Still, despite that overt display of affection, Gosling has always been something of a bashful creature. The Canadian actor is soft-spoken and giggle-prone. On-screen, he can ooze James Dean levels of brooding, like in *Drive*, where he turned a bomber jacket with a scorpion emblazoned on it into a cool dude calling card. However, find him out of character and he shrinks a little.

He's not the most gregarious of stars. He's intensely private about his relationship with Eva Mendes, the mother of his children. Half the time he seems almost embarrassed when he's out on the promotional trail for a project. Every so often, he's captured doing a good deed when he thinks there are no cameras watching, like the time he broke up a fight in New York City.

As time went on Gosling remained beloved by many, but his moment on the web has passed. The memedom of Gosling was a strange and fleeting period. He didn't have to do anything to become representative of the ideal sweetie pie of a man. He just was, and his admirers went to work.

A FIELD GUIDE TO INTERNET BOYFRIENDS

SEXY SUBJECT:

IDRIS ELBA

PLACE OF ORIGIN: London

NATURAL HABITAT: Brooding on a stormy day

ATTRIBUTES: Serious smolder, a touch of grey stubble, a sick collection of beats

When you think of Idris Elba's best roles, the ones that propelled him to Internet Boyfriend status, they tend to be very capital-S serious. There's Stringer Bell on *The Wire* and DCI John Luther in *Luther*. These parts create the notion of Elba as a charismatic and brooding figure, a poet of internal turmoil, smoldering as he considers the bleakness of the world around him.

But then there's the other Idris Elba. The Idris Elba who comes off as a dude who wants to have a damn good time as much as he wants to be a lauded actor. This is the Idris Elba who is a DJ, *and* who creates a Netflix series in which he plays an aspiring DJ. This is the Idris Elba who is appearing in *Cats* because he just really wanted to do a musical.

Elba's career is something of a conundrum, but his appeal is not. Whether he's engaging in sexually charged banter with a murderer on the BBC or playing house remixes of Lana Del Rey in Ibiza, he makes it work for him. Elba manages to be both devastatingly suave and just a little bit cheeky, and that combination proves persistently irresistible.

Perhaps film executive Amy Pascal said it best when speaking to the *New York Times* back in 2017. "He is like the best version of masculinity," she said. "All his complicated contradictions make every character he plays fascinating. Maybe it's the way he walks, like his legs are more powerful than anyone else, like he is gravity. He always seems like he is in the midst of a moral struggle, but he is the calmest one in the room. It's rare, undeniable movie star stuff."

Elba's path to movie stardom has been as offbeat as his own personality. The child of a father from Sierra Leone and a mother from Ghana, he grew up in Hackney, London, where he gained an interest in acting. As he waited for his big break after moving to the United States for his career, he DJ'd while working the door at Caroline's Comedy Club and selling weed on the side. When *The Wire* came along, he finally tasted American success, but the show was more popular in its afterlife than when it was actually on the air. It wasn't truly until *Luther* began airing in 2010, that the Elba fandom really gained steam. In between those he starred in *Obsessed*, a corny but very popular Tyler Perry thriller alongside Beyoncé, and did a stint on *The Office*, wherein he said the line that is basically the thesis of this essay. As the new boss in town Charles Miner, Elba deadpans: "I am aware of the effect I have on women."

Just what is that effect? Well, it's the sensation that comes over you when he bites his lower lip. Or maybe it's the way his coat moves in the breeze when he's trying to solve a case on *Luther*? Shirtless GIFs of Elba are legion, but you don't even really need to see skin—though of course it doesn't hurt. He can make a boring button-down with an unremarkable tie look like the hottest thing in the world, especially if, while he's donning that, he's in a sexually tense tête-à-tête with a serial killer played by Ruth Wilson. He was named *People's* "Sexiest Man Alive" for a reason, after all.

But Elba's unimpeachable hotness has always been something for him to have a fun with. He *knows* what he's doing when he flashes just a little smile or gives an exasperated glance. He's conscious of his power when Chrissy Teigen, ragging on her Sexiest Man Alive husband John Legend, challenges Elba to send a picture of himself in 1995 and the picture practically burns a hole in your screen.

It also speaks to the general way Elba moves through life and his, admittedly, sort of weird career. He's said—according to a *New York Times* profile way back in 2010—that he has no designs to only make prestige projects. "You can't afford to turn your nose up at things," he said. "Audiences want to see you a bit more dynamic. We know you can act, Daniel Day-Lewis. That's fantastic. Show us a bit more. We want to be entertained."

That's the thing: Idris Elba wants to entertain us. He wants to entertain us when he's Stringer Bell going head-to-head with Michael Kenneth Williams's Omar Little, and he wants to entertain us when he's blasting tunes from his DJ booth. Elba doesn't limit himself. He does a Marvel franchise. He gets freaky on a mountain with Kate Winslet in an adventure-romance. He plays Nelson Mandela. He cancels the apocalypse in *Pacific Rim*. And he does all this while pursuing other passions like music and comedy. Even in 2019—when he's a bona fide movie star—he creates and stars in a British sitcom about a Nigerian family that's different from his Netflix DJ sitcom. Yes, this man has two (two!) sitcoms.

But even though he's done all this, many agree there is one role he has yet to play that suits him best: James Bond. (The racist naysayers can, frankly, go straight to hell.) The reason we want to see Elba as Bond is because he looks great in a suit, yes, and also because it just seems like he'd have a really good time with it. He'd *lean in* to the character's beefcake status, the winking masculinity. He is, yes, aware of the power he has over women and would use that to his advantage.

Unfortunately, that ship has probably sailed, even though Elba has said he would certainly agree to playing the character should it ever come up. "Of course, if someone said to me 'Do you want to play James Bond?,' I'd be like, Yeah! That's fascinating to me. But it's not something I've expressed, like, Yeah, I wanna be the Black James Bond," he told *Vanity Fair*.

And just because the entertainment industry has a bad track record of making Idris Elba conform to its standards instead of conforming to his own doesn't mean the dream should stop there. Idris Elba doesn't *need* James Bond to make him seem like the pinnacle of sex appeal, so why is that the only role we can fantasy cast him in? Whither Elba's own version of Bond—or his John Wick for that matter—that isn't burdened by outdated ideas?

We'll just keep waiting. The joy of being an Elba fan is that he keeps surprising you. One moment he's plumbing the depths of the human soul, and the next he's spinning at Coachella, letting the beat drop as the crowd goes wild around him. Hell, fans of *The Wire* might have been under the impression he was American until he started speaking in his dulcet British tones. Idris Elba resists categorization, and that makes him stand out.

A FIELD GUIDE TO INTERNET BOYFRIENDS

SEXY SUBJECT:

CHRIS EVANS

PLACE OF ORIGIN: Boston

NATURAL HABITAT: On a couch with his dog

ATTRIBUTES: Tight ass, tighter sense of social justice

There's a GIF that left an indelible mark on the history of the internet. A GIF of an ass. Chris Evans's ass to be specific. It comes from a scene in 2012's *The Avengers*. Evans, as Captain America, is wailing on a punching bag, and the camera zooms in on him from behind. For a brief moment you get an unbroken shot of the butt. It jiggles ever so slightly as his fists go into the bag. It's a moment that turns the male gaze on an object of masculinity. It's one that made eyes across the world do that cartoon thing where they pop out of their skulls.

The fervor over Captain America's ass grew so loud over the years that when it finally came time to bring one chapter of the Avengers saga to a close with *Avengers: Endgame*, writers Christopher Markus and Stephen McFeely decided that they just had to acknowledge the posterior. Not to get too in the weeds with the wonky time travel plot of *Endgame*, but members of the superhero team go back in time to 2012 in order to stop Thanos's plan from ever happening. Ant-Man, fellow Internet Boyfriend Paul Rudd, crowns old Cap's behind as "America's ass," a title that Cap himself happily assumes. You see, Marvel and Evans himself just had to respond to the ogling.

It's not fair to reduce the internet's affection for Evans into a GIF of his butt, even though the butt GIF is significant. Of all the Hollywood Chrises—and we debated for a while which one to include here—Evans is the most representative of the Internet Boyfriend virtues.

Here's the thing: It wasn't always this way. It took some time for Evans to break out of the mold of your average hot white guy. Before he was inducted into the Marvel Cinematic Universe, his looks pigeonholed him. In *Not Another Teen Movie* he embodied the parody of an attractive jock. In *Scott Pilgrim vs. The World* he was a (very funny) parody of a ridiculously hot evil ex-boyfriend. In *Fantastic Four*, his first stab at being a superhero, he was muted by the blandness of the movie itself. I'll admit that when he took on the role of Steve Rogers in *Captain America*, I wasn't all that excited. Captain America? Snooze, I thought. Easily one of the most boring superheroes, a soldier frozen in time. And Evans? Seriously, I thought, we already gave that guy a chance to be a movie star and it didn't work out? Evans—if viewed in a vacuum—looks like the model of an All-American handsome dude, and what's the fun in that? Where's the edge?

I, of course, was wrong about Evans. (I also hadn't seen his angry performance in the underrated sci-fi movie *Sunshine* yet.) First of all, Evans has plenty of edge. His portrayal of Cap is far from boring. Instead, his nobleness and loyalty get taken almost to a fault. He's stubborn and wry, and 100 percent in love with his friend Bucky. (If you would like to debate that point, take it up with Tumblr.)

But Evans's place in our hearts was cemented by his off-screen behavior during his tenure in the Marvel Cinematic Universe. As the years went on, Evans got more politically engaged and subsequently more attractive to those who follow him. During the early days of his Marvel promotional interviews he came off as a genial beer-drinking bro, a mama's boy from Boston, like the second coming of Matt Damon. (See, for instance, his 2011 *GQ* cover, which depicts the reporter's wild night getting trashed with Evans.) As time passed, he maintained that good-time guy demeanor, but added a socially conscious streak to his persona. He called President Trump a racist. He (rightfully) declared a Straight Pride Parade in Boston homophobic. He started a website with the notion of helping the public become better informed on political issues. It got made fun of for being maybe a little too nonpartisan in these divided times, but Chris's heart was in the right place.

Evans ended up being the right kind of woke bae: supportive, but conscious of his place in society as a white man. In a 2018 *New York Times* profile, he discussed his efforts to be a good ally and shut the hell up sometimes. When he was dating the comedian Jenny Slate, she introduced him to Rebecca Solnit's *The Mother of All Questions*. He cited that book to the *Times* proving that he's not only the kind of boyfriend who will read the books you recommend, but also someone who will take them to heart.

Though they are no longer together, the Slate connection did wonders for Evans. By linking up with one of the funniest people alive who also has the demeanor of just another girl in Brooklyn, he gave hope to millions of women with frizzy hair who believed they too could have an Evans in their lives. Evans, it's obvious, has a sense of humor about the world and himself. He even called in to the podcast Thirst Aid Kit to talk about why people desire him—yet another move that proves just how good-humored he is.

Chris Evans seemingly has the bearing of an excited Labrador retriever—so much so that one Twitter account even made it its mission to find photos of him that matched up with derpy images of pups. Thus, it only makes sense that he loves dogs. Evans's obsession with his rescue dog Dodger is one of his most Internet Boyfriend-esque traits. His Twitter account is full of pictures of Dodger and tales of Dodger's antics—like Dodger's obsession with a singing lion toy. The constant stream of dog-related content again brings Evans's image back down to earth. The trappings of superhero celebrity slip away when you just think of him as a dude that's genuinely devoted to his dog so much so that he'll talk about poop online.

Endgame didn't just mark the crowning of Evans's butt as "America's ass," it also put a fine point on his time as Steve Rogers. By the end of the film, he's withered and aged and passes off the shield to Anthony Mackie's Falcon. Becoming Cap made Evans an Internet Boyfriend, but leaving him behind might solidify his place in the celebrity crush pantheon. Without the Marvel attachment Evans is liable to get weird. He's already done so in *Knives Out*, playing a charismatic jerk in luxurious sweaters and thereby birthing even more iconic GIFs. (Check out the ones of him saying "wow" and "eat shit.") He's spoken about his desire to direct more. He'll hopefully have more time to spend with Dodger. The ass may have been the reason the world took notice of Evans, but he's far more than just a nice butt.

A GUIDE TO THE HOLLYWOOD CHRISES

No name has carried more weight in discussion of celebrity crushes in the twenty-first century than "Chris." Chris! Often short for Christopher, as in Saint Christopher! Derived from the Greek *Christophoros* meaning "bearing Christ!" Also it's the name of a bunch of actors who rose to fame in the mid-2000s. Is there one way to define the Chrises? Well, they are mostly white. They are mostly buff. They are mostly blonde. They often play superheroes or superhero-esque figures. The fact that so many Chrises—cast in so many similar roles—rose to fame around the same time is both amusing and frustrating. Hollywood was looking for a type, and these guys fit the bill.

OTHER CHRISES OF NOTE:

Chris Messina (*The Mindy Project* bae)

Christopher Meloni ("These are their stories" bae)

Chris Rock (comedy legend bae)

Chris Noth (Big bae)

Chris O'Dowd (Irish *Bridesmaids* bae)

CHRIS
EVANS

SUPERHERO ALIASES: Captain America and the Human Torch, though we choose to forget about the latter.

DEFINING ASSET: Uh, his ass. (As in, America's ass.)

PERSONALITY TRAITS: Affable, woke.

PLACE OF BIRTH: Boston. But he's not a Masshole.

IS HE AN INTERNET BOYFRIEND? Yes.

CHRIS
PRATT

SUPERHERO ALIAS: Star-Lord

DEFINING ASSET: The abs which once weren't

PERSONALITY TRAITS: Used to be a sort of paunchy funny guy, now takes himself way too seriously.

PLACE OF BIRTH: Virginia, Minnesota, raised in Washington

IS HE AN INTERNET BOYFRIEND? No. Andy Dwyer was. Current Chris Pratt is not.

CHRIS PINE

SUPERHERO ALIAS: He's actually a superhero sidekick, playing Steve Trevor to Gal Gadot's Wonder Woman. He's also Captain Kirk in the *Star Trek* movies, who is certainly heroic if not superheroic.

DEFINING ASSET: Those baby blue eyes

PERSONALITY TRAITS: He's well read, does theater, and is the thinking woman's Chris.

PLACE OF BIRTH: Los Angeles

IS HE AN INTERNET BOYFRIEND? Yes, especially when singing or being second fiddle to a strong woman.

CHRIS HEMSWORTH

SUPERHERO ALIAS: Thor

DEFINING ASSET: His torso.

PERSONALITY TRAITS: Quick with jokes, aware of his godlike looks.

PLACE OF BIRTH: Melbourne, Australia

IS HE AN INTERNET BOYFRIEND? Yes, but only when he's goofy.

SEXY SUBJECT:

HENRY GOLDING

PLACE OF ORIGIN: Malaysia

NATURAL HABITAT: Touring around some gorgeous locale

ATTRIBUTES: Classic style, kind eyes, sense of adventure

Henry Golding arrived, seemingly out of nowhere, and was instantly a huge movie star. Unlike so many people in this book, he doesn't really have a tale of working his way up in the industry through a series of mildly humiliating bit parts. He never played Hot Guy #1 or Helpful Barista with No Lines in some middling early 2000s teen comedy. Instead, he was ushered into our lives to be an Internet Boyfriend and an Internet Boyfriend he became.

Director Jon M. Chu had a difficult task when he was adapting the best-selling novel *Crazy Rich Asians* into a movie. He had to find someone to play the perfect man. In Kevin Kwan's book Nick Young is sort of, well, *everything*. He's impossibly handsome, incredibly smart, and casually worldly. And, yes, he's secretly very very wealthy, but also humble about that wealth. On-screen, the actor playing Nick had to embody all of that. He also had to be Asian, obviously, and thanks to Hollywood's habit of whitewashing everything that comes across its path, the industry had to look beyond its usual collection of Chrises for actors that fit the bill.

A worldwide search was underway to find someone who could possibly play Nick. But when Chu discovered Golding, it was like the clouds parted, the light of heaven emerged, and this ideal candidate appeared. How had he not always been in our lives?

What's so good about Henry Golding? Well, first things first, he's a man of many talents. He initially—before the movie or even TV stardom—was a hairdresser. So, yes, you can fantasize about him running his hands through your locks. He can also show you the world. His next job was as a travel presenter for the BBC and Discovery Channel. Watch any of the videos from his days showing people how to navigate places like Kuala Lumpur, and you'll want to grab your passport, throw on a backpack, and head to the airport. He could convince even the biggest couch potato—read: me—to become an adventurer.

He was in the midst of that career when an accountant working on *Crazy Rich Asians* in Malaysia told Chu about this very attractive TV host. As the story goes, Chu then stalked Golding on social media and brought him in for an audition. To hear Chu explain it, Golding was just a total natural. "He's like John F. Kennedy Jr. in New York, cooler than any of these [other] guys we were reading, and he's not even trying," the director told *The Hollywood Reporter* at the time. Must be nice to be just that gosh darn naturally talented.

His casting, it should be noted, was the source of some controversy, as he is the child of an English father and Malaysian mother. He even handled that just about as well as he could, saying: "I think it's definitely a conversation that should be seen because it kind of just shows the studios that we're watching [that] we're very aware of how we want our films to tell authentic stories."

In the movie, Nick is the boyfriend of our heroine Rachel Chu, a Chinese American NYU professor. He's her colleague with a smooth British accent, who is also, it turns out, the scion of one of the wealthiest families in all of Asia. Making Nick a believable love interest is not the easiest task in the world. After all, he's someone who deliberately does not reveal a key facet of his history to his long-term girlfriend before throwing her into a situation he knows will be difficult: traveling to Singapore for his best friend's wedding wherein she'll meet his highly critical mother. Refinery29 even asked at some point: "Is Nick Young from *Crazy Rich Asians* a Bad Boyfriend?" But you forget all about that when watching Golding. All of Nick's slight cluelessness as to the extraordinary nature of his situation dissolves when Golding smiles with his slightly askew teeth. (So British! How charming!) He offers an ideal fantasy: a man desperately in love with you who can also provide everything you want without being obnoxious about it.

The *Crazy Rich Asians* press tour further cemented that Golding himself didn't do anything to break the spell the role cast. In interviews, he was thoughtful and charming, declaring his love for Shake Shack burgers. Photo shoots cast him as a romantic lead from days gone by, dressing him up in the mid-century aesthetic of fellow dreamboat Tony Leung in Wong Kar-wai's quintessentially gorgeous film *In the Mood for Love*.

His Instagram account furthers the impression of his blessed life. He's constantly in some beautiful locale with "love of [his] life" wife Liv Lo, another TV host and fitness instructor. He knows that it's just good sense to pose with a dog in a sweater.

But Golding was also quick to establish that his Hollywood career would not be limited to one role. He was Blake Lively's dreamy but mysterious husband in *A Simple Favor* and a captivating ghost in the holiday rom-com *Last Christmas*. In an age when rom-coms and movies aimed at women are still few and far between, Golding has happily made a career of being a female object of desire, emulating fellow Brits like Hugh Grant and Colin Firth. (Their initial rise as ideal Internet Boyfriend material predates the internet, but we'll go ahead and look at GIFs of Firth emerging out of the water in the *Pride and Prejudice* miniseries any day.) Those aren't the only roles Golding will ever play, certainly. For one, he's doing a G.I. Joe spin-off—a film that likely will not have the female gaze too much in mind. But the fact that he launched his career in a genre that's been so derided, especially by men, has solidified him as an Internet Boyfriend.

The beauty of a rom-com is suspension of disbelief. The man of the heroine's dreams arrives and it's just a little too perfect, but you give in to the swoony pleasures. Henry Golding's mere existence as a celebrity feels like a rom-com come to life.

SEXY SUBJECT:
JAKE GYLLENHAAL

PLACE OF ORIGIN: Los Angeles

NATURAL HABITAT: Near a weird-looking cat

ATTRIBUTES: Piercing blue eyes, wacky behavior, gold chain around neck

When did you realize Jake Gyllenhaal was a gosh darn freak? There was plenty of evidence. His moodiness in *Donnie Darko* all those years ago; that time he bounced around in short shorts in the Bong Joon Ho movie *Okja* after a string of outré appearances that could be described as Nicolas Cageian; the fact that he may or may not run an Instagram account dedicated to a cat named Ms. Flufflestiltskin?

If you weren't paying attention to Gyllenhaal's pivot toward the flamboyant, you might have gotten wind of it watching Internet Boyfriend John Mulaney's Netflix special *John Mulaney & the Sack Lunch Bunch*. Gyllenhaal bursts onto the screen in the last minutes of the show as Mr. Music. He wears a xylophone vest and has a breakdown as he tries to prove that you don't need an instrument to make music. It's unhinged. And it's why we love Jake. Whenever it was, you should be aware by now that Jake Gyllenhaal is a giant weirdo.

It didn't always seem this way. For a while there, Gyllenhaal seemed like a regular inordinately hunky actor. He came of age as a wide-eyed youngster with a bit of an edge. He forever became an avatar for disaffected youth with *Donnie Darko*, which he starred in alongside his sister Maggie. ("Oh, dear Elizabeth, how does one suck a fuck?") He officially became the person we just couldn't quit when he appeared opposite Heath Ledger in *Brokeback Mountain*.

But then, for a while, he was giving the old traditional movie star thing a go. He even got ripped and shirtless and culturally insensitive in *Prince of Persia: The Sands of Time*. He got maple lattes with Taylor Swift and inspired her best song ever. (It's "All Too Well." Please do not fight me. I am right.)

But sometime around 2013 and 2014 he started to commit fully to weirdness. He gave intense, unsettling performances in movies like *Nightcrawler*, where he transformed himself into a bug-eyed local news cameraman, eager to capture disaster at any turn. But unlike some "serious actors"—cough, Joaquin Phoenix—Gyllenhaal mostly seemed to be having a ton of fun in his work.

Okja is arguably the peak of this. Playing the mouthpiece for a corporation that genetically engineers adorable "super pigs" with the aim of turning them into human snacks, he wears a tricked-out safari outfit with oversize glasses. He's big and broad and rivals Tilda Swinton for the person doing the "most" in the movie. (I personally think he wins, *despite* the fact that she's playing twins.)

And then, he started doing musicals. If there's a surefire way to win the internet over, it's to sing. (See: Oscar Isaac.) If you want to guarantee a lifetime of love, do the following: Sing Sondheim. (See: Adam Driver in *Marriage Story*.) Surely, deciding to perform in a production of *Sunday in the Park with George* was not a calculated move to endear himself to the strong coterie of nerds online, but it did so nonetheless. Because Gyllenhaal's dabbling in the world of musical theater wasn't just vanity—he was actually *really* good at it. And, yes, it turns out that Gyllenhaal, as Georges Seurat, singing about art, can melt your heart.

By 2019, Gyllenhaal started letting the eccentricity of his choices slip into his public demeanor. It wasn't that he stopped caring. It was that he stopped being guarded at all. At the Sundance Film Festival, where he was promoting the high art slasher film *Velvet Buzzsaw*, in which he played a vaping art critic named Morf—yes, Morf—he set Twitter ablaze during an otherwise rote media appearance. When his director Dan Gilroy horribly mispronounced the word *melancholy* as something like "melankly," Gyllenhaal deadpanned, "It's melancholy, Dan." Was it an inside joke? Was he really just fed up? It doesn't really matter. His blunt retort was refreshing and meme-worthy.

His lack of filter seemed to follow him all year, even when on the press tour for a much bigger film: *Spider-Man: Far From Home*, in which he was Mysterio, a villain with a flair for theatrics. He wore a gold chain to nearly every media appearance. He acted as big brother to his younger costar, and burgeoning Boyfriend, Tom Holland.

He went ballistic about Sean Paul. What? Yes. Sean Paul. Gyllenhaal and Holland were doing a segment for BBC Radio 1 called "Unpopular Opinions." When a caller declared the Jamaican rapper Sean Paul to be "massively overrated," Gyllenhaal took great offense. "No, absolutely," he bellowed. "Sean Paul makes every song better he's in." When the DJ puts on Sia and Sean Paul's "Cheap Thrills," Gyllenhaal fully and completely gets into it, pumping his fist and grooving out. The excitement he showed was revelatory. Who knew Gyllenhaal could get extremely jazzed about the guy who sang "Temperature"?

These twin anecdotes offer the two poles of Jake Gyllenhaal, Weirdo. He's always either just a touch salty or a hair overenthusiastic. But really the crowning moment in the most recent run of weirdness was his association with the @ms.flufflestiltskin Instagram account. Fluff, as we'll call her for brevity's sake, is a flat-faced cat that may or may not belong to Jake Gyllenhaal. Whether or not she does, he seems to have a vested interest in her and she in him. He follows her. She dresses up as him. It's a mutual relationship. Just *how* Gyllenhaal is connected to Fluff remains a mystery, but the fact that he *is* involved with a meme-making cat is really all you need to know. If there's one thing more internet than an Internet Boyfriend, it's an Internet Famous Cat.

At this point, it seems clear that Jake Gyllenhaal will continue to make films that win him acclaim as an actor. Hell, given his range of talents he could probably even EGOT one day. But for every prestigious film he makes, I hope he'll continue letting his freak flag fly. Every Oscar-worthy performance deserves something like Mr. Music. There's something endlessly compelling about someone as attractive as he is being willing to make himself look utterly foolish for our own entertainment. Keep Jake Gyllenhaal weird.

OSCAR ISAAC

PLACE OF ORIGIN: Guatemala City

NATURAL HABITAT: Strumming a guitar in a cityscape

ATTRIBUTES: Great singing voice, great dance moves, chiseled jaw, prominent thighs

Where to start with Oscar Isaac? Is it the singing? For simplicity's sake, let's start with the singing. Oscar Isaac sings. And he sings well. The first time most of us really sat up and took notice of him was when we saw him play the title character in the Coen brothers' *Inside Llewyn Davis*. Llewyn, a folk singer haunting New York in the 1960s, is a complete shitheel of a human being. He abuses the kindness of everyone around him, mired in his own ambition and subsequent failures. But then he sings—and *oh* how he sings. That's the conundrum of the film: Llewyn is a talented musician who will never succeed. But the audience can appreciate his gifts, and, in turn, the gifts of Oscar Isaac. When he is strumming and crooning, it's hard not to become smitten.

If you are anything like me, you then dove down the "Oscar Isaac singing" YouTube rabbit hole. Maybe you found the scene from the mostly forgotten movie *10 Years*, in which his character serenades Kate Mara's with "Never Had," a song that Isaac wrote himself. Maybe you then encountered a clip of Isaac on a Brooklyn rooftop performing a tune from his band NightLab. Maybe eventually you hit on the time he did an acoustic cover of Katy Perry's "Roar" on *Late Night with Jimmy Fallon*. Or you discovered—and promptly decided to forget about—his ska career. (Just the same way you might have stumbled upon that picture of him wearing an Ayn Rand shirt and decided to conveniently ignore that too. It's fine. He's said he doesn't agree with her politics.)

Okay, okay: But maybe it's not the singing. Maybe it's the dancing. Let's consider the dancing for a moment. In 2014's *Ex Machina*, Isaac plays another character who, without mincing words, is an asshole. Nathan is a tech god who builds robots with hot female bodies and gives little thought to their emerging consciousnesses. But he boogies—*oh* how he boogies. As tension rises in the narrative, Isaac's Nathan turns on a red light and does a choreographed disco with one of his creations, played by Sonoya Mizuno. He is wearing a sweatshirt with nothing underneath that remains largely unzipped as he sways his hips. It's a lot. It didn't matter that, in context, it was highly disturbing. That's the power of Isaac's bare chest and formidable moves. The scene became a meme.

That's not the only time Oscar Isaac has danced though. Are you kidding? Of course it's not. One time, on the set of *Star Wars: The Force Awakens*, he led a veritable army of Resistance fighter pilots in a chorus line. The GIF has become so ubiquitous that it almost seems like it was in the movie. It was not.

Fine. Oscar Isaac's charm could be the singing. It could be the dancing. It could be that time he ate Hot Cheetos with chopsticks while wearing a beanie. (Have you seen that image? If you have not: Google. Now.) Or it could be that Isaac, even as he has transformed from indie breakout to *Star Wars* hunk, comes off perpetually as just one of the most talented men in the business who also seems like just a delight to be around: good-humored even as he smolders.

Before becoming a movie star Oscar Isaac—née Óscar Isaac Hernández Estrada—was a sort of creative polyglot. According to a *Rolling Stone* profile, he wasn't the kind of capital-A actor who knew from infancy he wanted to go to Juilliard—which he eventually did. He was born in Guatemala and moved around the United States as a kid, eventually landing in Miami. He was a troublemaker and class clown, who at one point told his classmates that he was from Russia, even though he has no Russian ancestry. Before he decided to commit to acting he tried out that aforementioned ska career while also working as an orderly who sometimes dealt with dead bodies. But his innate gifts were undeniable. Almost as soon as he was finished with the conservatory program, he landed the role of Romeo in a Shakespeare in the Park production of *Romeo and Juliet*. He had small roles in big movies for about six years before *Inside Llewyn Davis* came along.

But Isaac probably wouldn't have reached full Internet Boyfriend potential if he hadn't landed the role of Poe Dameron in the new *Star Wars* trilogy. Before he was Poe, he was best known for prickly characters in arty films. Poe gave him an opportunity to be a perfectly coiffed but also somehow rugged adventurer in the mold of his predecessors like Harrison Ford. The cast of *Episode VII: The Force Awakens* was a veritable murderer's row of Internet Boyfriends and Internet Boyfriends to be. Adam Driver was the moody one as Kylo Ren. John Boyega brought wide-eyed innocence to former stormtrooper Finn. But Oscar Isaac's Poe Dameron was arguably the dreamiest new addition to the cast, putting the star in Estar Guars. (On the *Tonight Show* Isaac explained that's how his fanboy uncle, who he brought to the set of *Force*, defines the series. Said relative also made "Estar Guars" shirts for the cast.)

Poe is a pilot with a cocky side and a glint in his eye. He has undeniable sparks with basically everyone who crosses his path from Carrie Fisher's General Leia to droid BB-8. His relationship with Boyega on screen and off was a particular flash point. In the first moments of *The Force Awakens*, Poe takes Finn under his wing. They are soon separated, but their ultimate reunion is the stuff of romantic melodramas given how flushed with emotion it is. Fan fiction writers were ignited.

Boyega and Isaac knew they had something on their hands and started to milk this bromance tinged with sexual tension for all it is worth. (On the press tour for the final film in the new trilogy, *The Rise of Skywalker*, Isaac expressed disappointment that Finn and Poe were never explicitly written as gay. Boyega later posted an Instagram of Isaac, in a bathroom, wearing a t-shirt with their faces. "I'm ready," Isaac says. "Let's do this.") Bromances—or simply friendships with people of any gender—are another one of Isaac's specialties along with singing and dancing. He developed a heartwarming intergenerational friendship with Carrie Fisher before her untimely death. He bit his pal Pedro Pascal's ear on Instagram. It's hard to deny that Isaac is a person who seems nice to hang around.

The magic Oscar Isaac works is in his medley of talent and personable good vibes. You know he's going to bring it whether he's flying an X-Wing or moping through the streets of New York in a project, but the promise of just chilling with him is endlessly attractive. It's just so easy to picture a jam session with Hot Cheetos and good buds.

OTHER *STAR WARS* BOYFRIENDS

A long time ago, in a galaxy far, far away . . . there was a war between good and evil that was seemingly never-ending. It involved Jedi and Sith and sometimes Gungans. We here on Earth watched it play out in nine movies over the course of nearly forty years, and in that time we developed some debilitating crushes.

THE CLASSICS

To paint a picture of the universe of *Star Wars* crushes, I must start with the o.g. ones: Harrison Ford and Carrie Fisher. Sure, the original trilogy came out before the internet was a thing, but, surely, if Tumblr had been around, it would have been all about GIFs of Han Solo and Princess Leia. Actually, I should rephrase: The fact that Tumblr is still full of GIFs of Han Solo and Princess Leia says it all. In recent years, nostalgia for hunky Ford has only gotten stronger. "The Internet Is Swooning Over Photos of Young Harrison Ford," *Time* magazine wrote in 2017. Meanwhile, Carrie Fisher, may she rest in peace, had a voice that flourished on the internet. She was the unequivocal star of *The Force Awakens* press tour, tweeting in her own special emoji language and bringing her French bulldog Gary everywhere. Fisher's return to the public sphere brought new appreciation for her entire career, her incredible writing, and the fearless way in which she addressed mental health. We also cannot forget Billy Dee Williams, aka Lando Calrissian, the ultimate smooth talker. (Donald Glover kept the legacy of Lando alive in *Solo*, even if the rest of the movie was pretty mediocre.)

THE LIGHT SIDE

With a nod to Natalie Portman's Padmé Amidala, I'm mostly going to skip right over the prequels, which did not have as strong crush energy. Now, no matter how you think the recently concluded sequel trilogy turned out, you must admit that Lucasfilm chair Kathleen Kennedy packed the cast with newcomers for Twitter to stan. I've already written at length about Oscar Isaac, but I must pay tribute to his better half: John Boyega. Boyega and Isaac make quite a team on a press tour, leaning into their natural banter with a ton of winks. Boyega's joyful Instagram presence, which directly ignores or rebukes some of the offensive trash that's been sent his way, is just more reason to love him.

THE DARK SIDE

There were many factors that led Adam Driver to take over the internet. But one that must be acknowledged is that moment in *The Last Jedi* in which he appears with high-waisted pants sans shirt. It's an image that launched a thousand memes, and some drool-worthy content. Driver's persona extends far beyond Kylo Ren. He's an object of fascination because of his intensity. (He used to eat an entire chicken for lunch when he was a student at Juilliard and run five miles to school every day.) His large features are perplexing but impossible to resist. He feels both dangerous and enticing, which is what makes him such an appealing villain, whether in space in *Star Wars*, or in Brooklyn on *Girls*. But, also, yeah, that shirtless shot.

We must also give an honorary mention to Kylo's internal foe: General Hux, played by Domhnall Gleeson. Gleeson has had much cuter roles (see, for instance, *About Time*), but his zany hysteria as Hux is adorable in its own way.

THE DROIDS

BB-8 is an Internet Boyfriend. Without question. Beep boop. Beep boop.

SEXY SUBJECT:

DWAYNE "THE ROCK" JOHNSON

PLACE OF ORIGIN: Hayward, California, but grew up in Hawaii

NATURAL HABITAT: Hanging off a building or something

ATTRIBUTES: Enormous muscles, flexible eyebrows, jolly demeanor

Looking back, it's funny to remember that Dwayne "The Rock" Johnson was ever supposed to be the heel. This guy? The nicest man in show business? The dude who just seems to want everyone to have a good time? He was supposed to be a bad guy?

Yes, really. If you remember way back to The Rock's WWE career, he was the superstrong man you were supposed to root *against*. He taunted people, in the third person, calling people "candy-asses" and raising that one eyebrow in that particular way. The Rock was the villain. I know, it's hard to believe, especially if you were never a wrestling fan. That's because The Rock's whole thing now is being widely liked. (Unless you're Vin Diesel, but that's another story for another time.)

Dwayne Johnson emerged from being a goofy villain in one of the most over-the-top corners of American entertainment into being everyone's favorite movie star, the dude you want to root for even if you are well aware that there's a high probability that his latest big-budget flick is kind of crappy. Johnson is the type of celebrity that could float the idea of a presidential run, and get a reaction like, "Well, that's kind of a funny joke, but you know, he also might actually unite the country, bringing us all together within the hug of his massive wingspan."

Sure, part of The Rock's appeal is that he looks like, well, a rock. He's a boulder of a person, whose muscle mass seems to only increase over time. But for as buff as Johnson is, he also comes off as sort of cuddly. Stay with me here. As his profile has risen, Johnson has also honed his teddy bear persona. An entire *GQ* profile of him was framed around the notion that, should you ever encounter Johnson in person, he would probably want to be your friend. He's an Internet Boyfriend, yes, but he's also an Internet Cheerleader, an Internet Camp Counselor, an Internet Overenthusiastic Sports Coach. With The Rock, it's not all about sexual attraction—though for some that is definitely the focus. But I'd venture to say that the main reason he's become a phenomenon on the internet and basically everywhere is not really lust-based. It's about wanting to be in the presence of someone who is so gosh darn gregarious you just can't help but feel a little warm and fuzzy inside.

That's why it's so funny that he started as a heel. Johnson came from a wrestling family, but he himself didn't really take off until one match when he found the audience jeering at his supposedly upbeat persona Rocky Maivia. He took that and spun it into gold, leaning into their negativity and emerging as a beloved hated figure. It's sort of the way he approached movies too. He made a mountain out of a molehill, turning a small role in *The Mummy Returns* into an opportunity to convince Universal that he deserves his very own vehicle with *The Scorpion King*.

His ascent as an actor was slow, and it arguably wasn't until he joined the *Fast and Furious* franchise in 2011 that his career—and the franchise itself—exploded. It's one of the reasons he has earned a reputation as "franchise Viagra," something he sang about during one of his *Saturday Night Live* monologues. Does your Hollywood property need a little boost? Add a sprinkling of The Rock. The *Fast* movies were a perfect match for him: Alternately bombastic and genial, they are about insane feats and also familia. He entered *Fast Five* once again as something of a villain, but his role quickly evolved into one of the heroes. That's just the way The Rock works. He can't stay bad for that long. It also might be that his off-screen persona can't help but infiltrate his on-screen one.

In everyday life he tries to conjure the image of a real-life superhero. Though he's newly remarried to his longtime girlfriend, he and his ex-wife are still on good terms—such good terms, in fact, that she produces all of his films. It's hard to picture The Rock without a smile on his face. He's often promoting some item that will benefit a charity, like the ice cream with proceeds going to Make-A-Wish or the clothing that will help military families in need. He's also made it known that he's—ah—committed to women's pleasure.

It's not that Johnson has somehow miraculously entirely evaded any sort of backlash, but he's also adept enough at bouncing back from his missteps that they don't really register. In his beef with *Fast* costar Vin Diesel—during which he called Diesel a "candy-ass" for his unprofessional behavior—Johnson came off looking like the party who was ostensibly in the right. And, yes, he betrayed a hint of conservative sympathies by calling young people "snowflakes," but on the other hand he's quite possibly Elizabeth Warren's favorite celebrity. She's one of the preeminent *Ballers* fans in the country.

There's obviously something inherently ridiculous about the very existence of Dwayne "The Rock" Johnson. This is a man that eats nearly two pounds of cod a day in order to look like a more handsome version of the demigod he voiced in *Moana* brought to life. And while there's something that reads both a little bit narcissistic and masochistic about someone so desperately committed to looking that unnaturally swole, Johnson counteracts that by being equally as committed to his public. You want him to sing? Oh, he'll sing. You want him to run for president? He'll consider it. (And then stop short of doing it because he realizes he's unqualified.) You want him to be a dork? He'll remind you of that time he wore high-waisted jeans in the '90s. You want him to be a bad guy? Sure, but just for a little bit and just because you want it. The Rock is not just your Internet Boyfriend. He's your Internet Champion.

MICHAEL B. JORDAN

PLACE OF ORIGIN: Newark, New Jersey, by way of California

NATURAL HABITAT: Your dreams

ATTRIBUTES: Shimmering abs, love of anime, easily memeable

The fantasy of Michael B. Jordan is so strong that women have gone out of their way to bring it to life. In April 2018, a girl did not have a date for prom so instead she took a life-size cutout of Jordan. She tweeted, it went viral, and Jordan invited her to the set of *Creed II*. In November of that year, a Twitter user named Bolu Babalola (@BeeBabs) posted a photoshopped image of herself alongside Jordan with the caption: "I met this guy on holiday this summer—we had a such a great connection but I changed my number and we lost touch. Twitter do your thing [crying emoji, prayer hands emoji, heart emoji]." The initial tweet was not a product of a delusional mind. The framing was tongue in cheek, but the love for this man was real. @BeeBabs also eventually connected with Jordan IRL. That's just the kind of guy he is.

It's no coincidence that both of these tweets happened in 2018. That was the year that Jordan went from a very attractive actor primed for global superstardom to actual global superstar thanks to his performance in *Black Panther*. Chadwick Boseman may have played the Marvel hero T'Challa, but it was Jordan who made the bigger impression as Erik Killmonger, the ostensible villain of the story even though the brilliance of Ryan Coogler's film was that Killmonger could just as easily be viewed as the protagonist. The image of Jordan as Killmonger was striking. In one moment he looked like a hipster with oversize glasses and a jean jacket, sweet-talking a museum curator and then issuing a threat merged with a lesson on colonialism. In another, he was shirtless and tattooed, bellowing, "Is this your king?" That line of dialogue became another meme, an easy way to be skeptical about something online, but it also solidified Jordan's status as royalty himself.

For almost his entire career—and it's been a long one—Michael B. Jordan has been part of major cultural moments. He was on two of the most beloved TV shows of all time, appearing as Wallace on *The Wire* and Vince Howard on *Friday Night Lights*. He successfully revived the *Rocky* franchise when he and director Ryan Coogler made *Creed*. And then came *Black Panther*.

Jordan is perhaps the only actor of his generation that approaches the platonic ideal of a movie star. He's handsome—obviously. I'm not sure that needed to be stated. Have you seen him? His shirtless and toned, oiled-up boxer-like physique in *Creed* inspired thirst GIFs for years to come. He can do just about anything: action, drama, and, while he's not as known for it, even comedy. (See: *That Awkward Moment*, which is not great, but a good hot guy delivery service.) And he chooses his projects carefully, with an eye toward social justice and responsibility. Speaking to *GQ* back in 2018, Jordan laid out his goals for his career. "I want to be worldwide," he said.

His idols? Tom Cruise, Will Smith, and Leonardo DiCaprio. He's already almost there.

While *Creed* may have been the film that proved he could lead a major studio franchise, it was Coogler's debut *Fruitvale Station* that served as his breakout. As Oscar Grant, the man who was murdered by a police officer on Oakland's BART in 2009, Jordan was as magnetic as he was heartbreaking. *Fruitvale Station* became a landmark documentation of an incident that inspired the Black Lives Matter movement, placing Jordan's work at the center of a national discussion. And as Jordan has gained more pull in Hollywood, he has shown a vested interest in telling stories and supporting projects that aim to make the world a better place—just one of the reasons we love him. He's someone who puts his money and his clout where his mouth is, making sure projects produced by his company Outlier Society have inclusion riders so that crews are diverse. Jordan is one of the few actors whose name is essentially a guarantee of goodness—both quality-wise and on a more spiritual level.

He's also used his platform to indulge his own nerdy obsessions. He's a big fan of anime, so he's executive produced his own, *gen:LOCK* for Adult Swim and turned a Coach collaboration into an homage to *Naruto*. ("I've definitely cried little man tears over anime before," he has said.) He also likes to have fun, clearly, and has a penchant for fooling around with his costars—particularly the *Black Panther* crew. (He and Lupita Nyong'o once staged an after-party photo booth make-out session that was interrupted by costar Danai Gurira in an elaborate gag for social media.) He's been notably elusive about his romantic life, but is a demonstrative good son. He lives with his parents and advocates for lupus research to help his mom, who suffers from the disease. He just seems like the type of guy that would charm the pants off your folks, while cracking a dirty joke just out of their earshot just to amuse you.

It's the dichotomy that Killmonger encapsulates. In the role, Jordan is simultaneously rebellious and righteous. He disrupts the order of Wakanda, and does so with verve and a cheeky smile. Jordan convinces you that the great tragedy of the movie is not that Killmonger challenges T'Challa, but that Killmonger doesn't win in the end. When he shouts "Is this your king?" we collectively say, "No, you are."

It just makes sense that people would go out of their way to bring Michael B. Jordan into their lives through cardboard cutouts and photoshopped tweets. If it pays off and he takes notice, you might learn that the reality is just as good as the fantasy.

SEXY SUBJECT:

DIEGO LUNA

PLACE OF ORIGIN: Toluca, Mexico

NATURAL HABITAT: Mexico City

ATTRIBUTES: Mischievous energy, small features, expertly groomed facial hair

If you haven't seen the supercut of Diego Luna wanting to touch Jabba the Hutt, please, I beg you, put down this book. Go to your computer. Go to YouTube, and experience true happiness. Here's how the story goes. When on the press tour for the *Star Wars* spin-off *Rogue One*, in which he played spy Cassian Andor, Luna just couldn't stop talking about how much he wanted to touch Jabba the Hutt, the thick, slimy villain from *Return of the Jedi*. At one point he's asked, as a joke, if he would French-kiss Jabba. After learning just what exactly French-kissing entails, he responds that he would without blinking. In another clip, he thinks about Jabba's texture. "It might be delicious," he says with an impish smile on his face. He's being completely serious. But that's just why we love Diego Luna: He's a risk-taker and always has been whether that comes to his work or, you know, his insatiable desire to feel one of the grossest characters in cinematic history.

Luna has dipped in and out of the limelight throughout his career, but whenever he emerges, he wins us over once again. Luna, from the moment we met him, had a mischievous air about him. This is why it seems prudent to start with his love of Jabba. (Or, if you pronounce it in his accent, "Yabba.") It's arguably the clip that launched him from well-respected/adorable actor into Internet Boyfriend status. It defies all logic, and yet somehow is totally endearing. It's pure Luna.

Of course, it would be inaccurate to discuss Luna completely independently. His ascent began as part of a duo. Alfonso Cuarón's film *Y Tu Mamá También* launched Luna and Gael García Bernal into public consciousness all at once. They played a pair of insatiably horny teenagers who go on a road trip across Mexico with an older woman who, unbeknownst to them, is dying. Luna is Tenoch, the richer and more childish of the two, while Bernal is Julio. Together, their energy and chemistry are electrifying. In the climactic scene their traveling companion leaves them alone to drunkenly consummate their erotically charged relationship. The GIFs of that scene live on in perpetuity.

The film was known for its gorgeous landscapes and those, yes, graphic sex scenes and made the two of them stars in the United States. It also established Bernal and Luna as a pair of sorts, inexorably linked by their friendship and their big break. But Luna was the one to make bigger moves toward a more traditional form of Hollywood stardom right off the bat.

For those who were maybe a little too young to see *Y Tu Mamá* when it was first released, but old enough to be susceptible to swoony romantic dramas in 2004, your first introduction to Luna might have been in *Dirty Dancing: Havana Nights*. The loose remake of the 1987 classic cast Luna in the same type of role occupied by Patrick Swayze in the original: He's the handsome, quote-unquote exotic man that our heroine (here played by Romola Garai) meets while on vacation, this time in Cuba. The movie was poorly received and did badly at the box office, but managed to make an impact on those who did see it, like the comedian and actress Awkwafina, who wrote *Havana Nights* into her character's masturbation routine on her sitcom *Nora from Queens*. As people like Awkwafina who saw *Havana Nights* at an impressionable young age grew into adults who could write blog posts and TV shows, appreciation for the movie—and specifically for Luna's charming turn as Javier, the waiter who turns the innocent American girl's life upside down—got more attention.

Luna flew almost under the radar for the next decade. He was known, yes, but he made films that were less likely to set the internet on fire. He continued working with Bernal on oddball projects, and even made a Harmony Korine movie where he played a Michael Jackson impersonator. It truly wouldn't be until *Rogue One* that Luna would win over the internet fully.

It wasn't just the Jabba stuff—though the Jabba stuff was a big part of it. *Rogue One* made us wonder why Luna wasn't in major blockbusters all the time. The movie, by its very nature, was a one and done thing. (Spoiler alert: They all die at the end.) But Luna did so well with a blaster that he got his own spin-off TV series for Disney+. The publicity, meanwhile, established Luna as a funny but also sincere voice. When a Tumblr user wrote a long post about how meaningful it was for her father to see Luna as a galaxy-hopping hero with a thick accent, he retweeted it, saying, "I got emotional reading this."

But he was always making radical moves. Just when he was reaching a new level of fame, he left Los Angeles and returned to his home in Mexico. Yes, Luna continued to work in big projects, like *Narcos*, but he devoted more of his time to activism. He's raised money for earthquake victims and started an organization called El Día Después aimed at combating racism and poverty, among other issues. He's even been floated as a potential political candidate in the country, though he dismisses that idea. "I have the role of being a citizen, which demands a lot from me," he told NPR.

Leaving the traditional idea of Hollywood was perceived as potentially damaging to his career, but Luna doesn't really seem to care. When asked about this by the *Los Angeles Times*, he casually said, "If they really need me, they'll come to me." And anyway that risk is one of the reasons we have consistently loved Luna all these years. He's an unabashed risk-taker. That can mean taking on a part like Tenoch in *Y Tu Mamá* or desperately wanting to touch Jabba the Hutt.

SEXY SUBJECT:

JASON MOMOA

PLACE OF ORIGIN: Honolulu, Hawaii

NATURAL HABITAT: The sea

ATTRIBUTES: Wild hair with a little bit of ocean spray, incredible enthusiasm

Everything Jason Momoa does is extreme. The man looks like a walking truck or beer commercial. He's in a state of perpetual ruggedness. His long mane flows to his shoulders with perfect beachy waves. It always seems like he either has ocean or beer spray in his beard. He digs motorcycles and heavy metal. You look at him and you can just hear a voice-over going: *For tough guys only.*

Even Momoa's enthusiasm is extreme. To tease the trailer for *Aquaman* he jumped off a cliff in his native Hawaii. Everything he says seems like it should be appended with three exclamation points. His declarations have a gusto that few others can muster. When he shouts "my man!" in the otherwise terrible *Justice League*, he bellows it in a manner that seems designed to knock you off your seat.

Momoa comes off like a cartoon version of a capital-D dude, entirely comprised of swagger. But the reason so many people are drawn to him is that underneath the pecs and all that exuberance lurks the heart of a big old sweetie pie, a guy who is just happy to be here.

Most of the viewing public sat up and took notice of Jason Momoa when he became Khal Drogo for the first season of *Game of Thrones*. But Momoa was playing a hunk long before that. He got his first break appearing at the tail end of *Baywatch*'s run, getting cast after attending the audition in

Hawaii just to meet some hot girls. He was baby-faced, short-haired, and perpetually shirtless. The acting was—as is typical of *Baywatch*—bad. He doesn't like to talk about that time much, referring to the notorious series known for jiggling beach runs as "the B-word," in a 2014 *Chicago Tribune* interview.

Still, it wasn't long before Momoa seemed bound for a career in cult TV shows. For years, he was Ronon Dex on *Stargate Atlantis*. Drogo on *Thrones* could have just as easily been a similar character, bound to appeal to Dungeons & Dragons devotees, hovering just below the mainstream. But *Thrones* became the biggest TV show on the planet, and Drogo became an object of lust.

The sexual politics of *Game of Thrones* are confusing, frustrating, and worthy of their own tome. The early seasons were full of exploitative material, mostly involving the naked female extras, solely there for titillation's sake. By all standards of modern feminism, Drogo should not have become a fan favorite. In early episodes, he was presented as a barbaric rapist, who used his new wife Daenerys Targaryen however he pleased. Over the course of that first season, Daenerys essentially trains Drogo, turning him to a faithful softy who sacrifices himself for her.

There's a lot to unpack in their love story: the nonconsensual nature of their initial interactions; the unfortunate stereotype of the noble savage tamed by a white woman. It's a credit to Momoa that the entire plot is remembered more as tragically romantic than deeply problematic. Despite having little dialogue—most of which was in Dothraki—he convinced audiences of Drogo's sensitive soul. He played into the admittedly fraught idea that a wild man can be deeply committed to the right woman.

He was only on *Thrones* for a short run, but that was all it took to make him a star. It was only a matter of time before he would become a superhero. He got the role of Aquaman in a casting that was a savvy rewrite of the typical image of the character. Instead of the clean-cut blonde Arthur Curry of the comic books, Warner Bros. found their new underwater hero in a POC—of Native American and Native Hawaiian descent, to be specific. While the less said about *Justice League* the better, his solo movie turned out to be giddy fun in part thanks to Momoa's up-for-anything interpretation of his character. Momoa's greatest gift as a performer is that he never looks like he's trying too hard. In action sequences, it seems like he could have strolled in from his personal beach day. The water, especially, seems to suit him. One gets the sense that he really does want to save the seas, and you'd be right—he does.

Before he was cast on *Baywatch*, he studied marine biology and wildlife biology in college in Colorado. He's made it his mission to try to keep the oceans clean. "Everyone just has no idea what you get to see firsthand when you live on an island," he told *Esquire* in a recent profile. "All the shit and garbage that rolls up. The rising of the tides." He wants everyone to use reusable water bottles to the extent that he's publicly shamed fellow superhero Chris Pratt for drinking out of plastic. "I'm just very passionate about this single-use plastic epidemic," Momoa said in his apology. "The plastic water bottles have to stop."

Momoa comes off as someone who loves the Earth and this blessed life he's gotten to live on it. He's over the moon that he married his onetime celeb crush, Lisa Bonet, showering her with near constant praise on the internet. He goes wild on Instagram when he gets sent Metallica merch or when he gets to go to a Slayer concert with his two kids. He's delighted when he runs into his costars like Emilia Clarke or Gal Gadot. (Sometimes his hype man status can go a little too far. We would like to have a talk with him about that time he tore pages out of his costar's book so she would pay attention to him.)

There are plenty of reasons why Jason Momoa has struck such a chord. Some of them are messy: With Drogo he projects an idea of exoticism that plays into troubling fantasies. Others are simple: He's really hot. But it's his boundless enthusiasm that's his biggest asset. You'd be happy to meet Jason Momoa, but he's probably happier to meet you.

SOME TV ZADDIES TO CONSIDER

TV and the internet are symbiotic, especially as streaming has become the dominant mode of viewing. Thus, shows have created zaddies.

ALL THE ADULTS ON *RIVERDALE*: Every adult man that has been cast on The CW teen show is a zaddy, including Mark Consuelos, Skeet Ulrich, and the dearly departed Luke Perry.

THE CAST OF *SUCCESSION*: The dudes of the Roy family are evil buffoons, but they are also zaddies.

MAD MEN'S MEN: Don Draper and Roger Sterling were not good men, but Jon Hamm and John Slattery earned forever spots on our zaddy list.

ALIAS DADDY; PERMANENT ZADDY: Victor Garber

GAME OF THRONES GUYS: Jason Momoa isn't the only GOT alumnus who has earned love. Don't forget Tyrion, Oberyn Martell, and even Bronn.

TONY SOPRANO: Bada bing.

GLENN ON *THE WALKING DEAD*: Steven Yeun! Duh!

STERLING K. BROWN ON *THIS IS US*: We're sobbing.

JOHN MULANEY

PLACE OF ORIGIN: Chicago

NATURAL HABITAT: New York, but like, in the 1970s

ATTRIBUTES: Suits, jokes, existential dread

Sometime in 2018, an eighteen-year-old girl figured out that John Mulaney punch lines could basically explain everything. A Twitter user named Anja Reese decided one day to post a thread in which she used quips from the comedian's specials to reference popular Broadway musicals. The tweets themselves have been lost to time, but she started a trend. Since then other fans have followed suit. Mulaney's words have been used to explain pop punk, classical music, athletes, and more. The threads, by their nature, are jokes upon jokes. If you get why Mulaney saying, "Yes, you heard me, an English major," describes Fall Out Boy, then this is for you.

These threads of Mulaney wisdom applied to other topics out of context are just one example of the way the stand-up has infiltrated the internet as a wholesome, sensible voice amid the noise. More than any other comedy persona, Mulaney represents the id of living online. His humor is both esoteric and universal. It's outwardly upbeat—he talks about politics only obliquely—while simultaneously being haunted by just a bit of existential dread. To watch or listen to John Mulaney is to contemplate being human.

Okay, that makes it all sound very *serious*. It's not. It's comedy after all—hyperarticulate, hyperliterate comedy, but still comedy. Still, whenever you finish spending time in his company, in whatever manner that may be, you end up feeling a little better than when you started.

It's hard to pinpoint when exactly the Mulaney hive started to evolve from a small but appreciative bunch into a widespread moment. Even Mulaney acknowledges he's a niche attraction. During an *SNL* monologue in early 2020 he joked: "I am like Louis Farrakhan. I mean a lot to a small group of people." For years, he was best known for his work behind the scenes on *Saturday Night Live*. Those who were in the know were privy to the fact that he was responsible for some of the funniest material coming out of Studio 8H. Without Mulaney, Bill Hader's Stefon would have never existed. Mulaney, as legend goes, would sneak jokes into the cue cards to make Hader break, which is why those sketches reached such a wonderful level of delirium.

A friend once observed, "I'm sure every thirtysomething woman feels like if she had met John Mulaney at the right moment, they'd be married now." It's an accurate assessment of his appeal: husband material. But crushing on John Mulaney is by its very nature theoretical. To love John Mulaney is to love how much he loves his wife Annamarie Tendler and their French bulldog Petunia. In his special *Kid Gorgeous*, one joke revolves around how Tendler allows him to make fun of her in his set, as long as he doesn't say she's a bitch and he doesn't like her. He retorts, "My wife is a bitch, and I like her a lot." It's devastatingly romantic in its bluntness. Every woman longs to have her power acknowledged by a man and be desired for that power.

There's something old-school and slightly gentlemanly about Mulaney, who sometimes seems like he was zapped in from a different era, be that the 1900s or the 1970s. Maybe it's the way his cadence can evoke that of a carnival barker or that he frequently references the likes of Leonard Bernstein, Stephen Sondheim, and Danny Aiello. Perhaps it's that, when he's doing stand-up, he's taken to wearing three-piece suits, a change from the frequently schlubby attire of many male comedians. A rare photo of Mulaney sans suit, taken backstage at *Late Night with Seth Meyers* alongside Andy Samberg in early 2020, created a frenzy online. Those of us who were aware that Mulaney was hot used it as further proof. For those who had not yet had that realization, the shot of Mulaney in glasses and a t-shirt with his hands in his pockets was all they needed.

But Mulaney is also weirdly good at *playing* an old person, adding to his vintage vibes. He and Nick Kroll made their Broadway debuts as characters George St. Geegland and Gil Faizon, two cantankerous Upper West Siders with liver spots who host a talk show called "Too Much Tuna." Gil and

George are, by design, terrible humans. A running joke is that George, played by Mulaney, is a serial killer. And yet, you're still charmed (I'm sure) to spend time in his company.

The darkness lurking in George is in a lot of Mulaney's material, and even in Mulaney himself at times. He hasn't hidden any of his own demons. He got sober when he was twenty-three and sometimes talks about his history of drug and alcohol abuse in his material. When fellow comedian Pete Davidson was working on his sobriety, Mulaney reached out, becoming a mentor to him and establishing an adorable odd couple funny guy friendship.

It's not just that Mulaney extends a hand to people in need, though. He also offers comfort in acknowledging that, yes, the world is pretty much a petrifying place. Take, for instance, his run about Detective J.J. Bittenbinder, a Chicago cop who would come talk to his elementary school, introducing kids to the concept of "stranger danger" and the terrors of leaving their homes. In his Netflix special *John Mulaney & the Sack Lunch Bunch*, a spin on *Sesame Street*-style TV programs, Mulaney interviews the young performers and his celebrity guest stars about their greatest fears. Silly musical numbers segue into discussions of mortality and therapy.

Mulaney's willingness to burst out into song—and make others do the same—is one of his most endearing traits.

Whenever he hosts *Saturday Night Live* these days, he brings with him a sketch inspired by musical theater set in a New York City location. The inaugural one was "Diner Lobster," in which a man orders the lobster off a menu at a diner, committing a faux pas designed to give him indigestion. But the gag is not only that it's very weird to order shellfish at a greasy spoon; instead it turns into the tragedy of the lobster himself, who comes to life and starts performing *Les Misérables*.

Ultimately, Mulaney is comedian as therapist. He introduces the *very* real notion that life is stressful and frequently grim, but talks you through it with sensitivity and erudition. That's why even his out-of-context quotes are so widely applicable. If you just let John Mulaney explain the world, everything will be okay.

FUNNY GUYS

Just a couple more of the comedy dudes who get us going.

ANDY SAMBERG: Really, everyone in the Lonely Island deserves a mention.

BILL HADER: Master of impressions; master of our hearts.

TAIKA WAITITI: On or off the screen, we love this weirdo in short-shorts and his quirky Kiwi sense of humor.

ZACH WOODS: Tall, disarmingly sexy, a tad deranged.

DAN LEVY: We'd move to Schitt's Creek for him.

BEN SCHWARTZ: Just try to tell us you wouldn't go for Jean-Ralphio even though he's the *wooooooorst*.

JASON MANTZOUKAS: A wild card we can't resist.

ANDREW RANNELLS: We're here for the quips and the amazing singing voice.

SEXY SUBJECT:

DEV PATEL

PLACE OF ORIGIN: Harrow, London

NATURAL HABITAT: The Los Angeles sun

ATTRIBUTES: Luscious hair, elusive personality, lovesick eyes

L et's just revisit some of the headlines about Dev Patel's hair: "The secret behind Dev Patel's luscious hair." "Can We Take a Moment for Dev Patel's David Copperfield Hair?" And, one that doesn't explicitly reference Dev Patel's hair, but might as well: "I, Too, Would Leave My Fiancé for Dev Patel." (The URL of that one is "dev-patels-hair-dazzles-in-modern-love" so it counts.) You see, sometime around 2016, Dev Patel, the boyish star of *Slumdog Millionaire*, grew his hair out. And heads turned.

Dev Patel certainly has more than just his hair going for him. He's evolved from excitable teen actor with a wide-eyed energy into a bona fide leading man, giving genuinely romantic performances all along the way. Still, his hair represents a turning point. Without the addition of some flowing locks, he likely would not have become an Internet Boyfriend.

Patel's career started—as many rising British stars' did—on *Skins*, the drama about a bunch of teens experimenting with drugs, sex, and all kinds of scandalous things. His mother encouraged him to audition, and he ended up with the part of Anwar, a Muslim boy from a devout family who has to hide his near uncontrollable horniness and otherwise wild behavior. He starred alongside other kids who would grow up to have fruitful careers: Nicholas Hoult, *Game of Thrones*' Joe Dempsie, and Jack O'Connell.

Patel's caught on earlier than any of theirs, though. Right after he finished *Skins*, he got the role that would define his career for better and worse for years to come. Director Danny Boyle had a daughter obsessed with *Skins*—as so many of us are in our adolescent years—who convinced him to cast Patel as the lead in *Slumdog Millionaire.* Patel came away with the role of Jamal, a young man in India competing on that country's version of *Who Wants to Be a Millionaire?* Jamal's success on the show ignites claims of cheating, but the film depicts how his difficult life and pursuit of his one true love lead him to the answers.

Slumdog Millionaire, admittedly, has aged poorly. There's a "poverty porn" aspect to its inspirational narrative—which was scripted and directed by two white men. What has stood the test of time is Patel's work. As Jamal, Patel did an incredible job of portraying the intense, years-long pining of his character for Freida Pinto's Latika. (The two ended up dating in real life for many years following the movie.) Oh, and did we mention his swoon-worthy moves in the Bollywood finale? One thing you might have forgotten about *Slumdog* is just how romantic it is. It established a precedent: Dev Patel pines better than almost anyone else in the game.

The movie launched Patel into global fame and won a ton of Oscars including Best Picture. But despite the work Patel had done carrying *Slumdog*, his contributions were almost underrated. He was outwardly frustrated with the roles he was offered afterward. "For my second film, I wanted a role that would stretch me, but all I was getting offered were stereotypical parts like the goofy Indian sidekick," he said in an interview. "Asian actors tend not to be sent Hollywood scripts that are substantial or challenging. I'm likely to be offered the roles of a terrorist, cab driver and smart geek. I want to show that I have versatility."

He held out and weathered some duds like M. Night Shyamalan's *Airbender: The Last Avatar*. But Patel refused to let Hollywood pigeonhole him into anything but a movie star. He made the best of Sorkinese in *The Newsroom* and charmed the grandes dames of British cinema in *The Best Exotic Marigold Hotel* and its sequel. The *Marigold Hotel* movies are two more that help build the case of Dev Patel being someone who is the absolute best at portraying being head over heels in love.

But 2016 represented a turning point for the actor. At the age of twenty-six, directors finally started realizing that Patel could do more than just embody the eager newbie. He appeared in *Lion*, the true story of a man, Saroo Brierley, who found his birth family in India using Google Maps. As Saroo, Patel created a portrait of a man wrestling with questions of identity—aware that his adoptive family in Australia brought him privilege, but understanding that there's something ineffably missing in his life. Nearly ten years after the Oscars had snubbed him for *Slumdog*, he finally received a Best Supporting Actor nomination.

The *Lion* press tour also introduced Patel's new look. The cropped cut was gone; the mane was in. The salivating blog posts were arriving, announcing his evolution from scrawny kid to bona fide heartthrob. Before the hair, Patel was a well-liked actor. After the hair, he was a Boyfriend. Vulture asked him what products he used to maintain it. The answer? A fairly shocking one. He just rubs Cetaphil moisturizer into his scalp. Yes, the same stuff he uses on his face.

Lion was the beginning of a new era for Patel, wherein directors have realized he doesn't need to be confined by any superficial labels. Armando Iannucci cast him as the Dickensian hero David Copperfield in *The Personal History of David Copperfield*, his adaptation of the novel, employing Patel's seemingly boundless persistence and integrity in this reinvention of the narrative. The Amazon series *Modern Love* put him in an episode based on the true story of a white dating app founder thinking about the girlfriend he let get away. (Again, with the heartsickness. If only he were thinking about . . . well, us.) David Lowery's *The Green Knight*, a new telling of *Sir Gawain and the Green Knight*, stars Patel as Gawain. The trailer sent shockwaves around Twitter when it opened with Patel, robe open and hair flowing, on a throne. A king indeed. These appearances ignited a whole new wave of Patel appreciation, and more stories about his hair.

But Patel is elusive. Unlike his peers he's not on social media. When he's not promoting a movie, he often stays out of the limelight. It's a small price to pay. It makes the moments we get with him—and his stunning hair—all the more special.

JOHN CHO

Hold on. I need to take a *Selfie*. Sorry, I need to *talk* about the short-lived ABC series *Selfie*, in which John Cho starred. Not many people saw *Selfie*. That's why it was canceled so soon after it began airing. But if you *did* watch *Selfie*, a sitcom loosely based on George Bernard Shaw's *Pygmalion*, you became aware that John Cho could convey more sexual tension in a single glance than most actors could in a full-blown sex scene. He played Henry Higgs, a new generation's Henry Higgins, who helps this Eliza—not a Cockney flower girl, but a social-media obsessed influencer with vocal fry. Their will-they-won't-they is scintillating.

Before *Selfie*, Cho was largely known as not a leading man but a sidekick. He was the stoned Harold in the *Harold & Kumar* movies and Sulu in the *Star Trek* reboot. He was successful in the broadest possible sense—he worked *a lot*—but there was a gnawing feeling that his potential was untapped. I mean, did you *see* how he looked at Karen Gillan in *Selfie*?

One man noticed how Hollywood wasn't taking advantage of the wealth of Cho's talent and turned him into a movement. William Yu started the hashtag #StarringJohnCho and photoshopped Cho's face into movie posters that otherwise featured white actors to make a point about the lack of Asian representation in Hollywood. It was 2016, and there had been a high-profile string of whitewashing cases. Emma Stone played a part-Chinese character in *Aloha*. Scarlett Johansson was cast as a classic anime hero in *Ghost in the Shell*. But Yu imagined a world where Asian actors weren't marginalized. What if Cho were James Bond? What if he were in the Avengers? What if he were a rom-com star?

#StarringJohnCho challenged the public's expectations of what a movie star looks like and opened up eyes to what a diverse entertainment industry could actually be. It also made us say, "Damn, John Cho." The reason the activism worked so well was in part because of the overwhelming charisma of Cho himself. Cho wore the movie star mantle so well that the powers that be would *have* to respond. #StarringJohnCho made John Cho an Internet Boyfriend overnight, forcing the public to realize that he's more than just that guy from those stoner movies.

In responding to the movement, Cho has been incredibly humble, which, of course, makes him even dreamier. He told the *New York Times*: "I'm sure to some extent #StarringJohnCho is a result of attitudes that were already shifting rather than changing minds on its own. But I'm grateful. I literally never thought I'd see the day."

Since #StarringJohnCho there have been more movies starring John Cho, including *Searching*, the first "mainstream thriller" (per the *Times*) starring an Asian American actor. In the indie *Columbus*, he gave one of the best dramatic performances of his career. He was cast as the lead in the live-action TV remake of the anime *Cowboy Bebop*.

To be honest, we're still waiting for the great John Cho romance movie. The one that will fulfill the promise of *Selfie* and capitalize on those gazes that make our bodies fully melt. This, at least, is a good start.

SEXY SUBJECT:

BILLY PORTER

PLACE OF ORIGIN: Pittsburgh

NATURAL HABITAT: Broadway

ATTRIBUTES: Fabulous outfits, inspiring confidence, incredible legs

I barely need to describe Billy Porter's most incredible sartorial moments for you to conjure them in your mind. There's the velvet tuxedo gown he wore to the Oscars with a bustle like something out of a nineteenth-century period piece. Or you might remember the form-fitting gold bodysuit accompanied by wings and a headdress that was his guise for the Met Gala's "Camp" edition. Note, too, that he entered the grand museum on a platform carried by six burly men. One time, at the Tonys, he wore an actual curtain. Porter steps out in tulle and rainbow patterns. He's worn a hat featuring a veil that opens on cue thanks to a microcontroller. When he goes to an event, he becomes the event.

In recent years the multitalented singer, director, and actor has established himself as the human embodiment of fabulousness. But it's not just that he looks great. Billy Porter has become legendary because of his glorious commitment to being exactly who he is, no matter who says anything. It seems trite to even call him to an Internet Boyfriend. While we love him, he is something more than that. He is the Internet's Conscience and the Internet's Savior all at once.

For most Broadway fans, Billy Porter's presence became impossible to ignore in 2013, when he started playing Lola in the musical *Kinky Boots*, about a British factory owner who begins making footwear for drag queens. Lola was the kind of showy part that often draws attention. Porter strode onto the stage in tight dresses and thigh-high boots belted with impressive might. But in a role that could be cartoonish, he brought depths of humanity to Lola.

Five years later, Porter is finally in a position where people beyond the cozy world of theater nerds are taking notice. That is largely thanks to *Pose*, the groundbreaking television show where his words—"the category is . . ."—kick off every episode. Creator Ryan Murphy knew he wanted to showcase Porter in a key role, but the one he ended up getting, Pray Tell, had not been invented when the pilot was being cast. Because of Porter's talent and experience with the material, Murphy ended up writing it just for him. The show chronicles the ball culture in New York City during the 1980s. Balls were places where largely Black and Latinx LGBTQ people could find community and glamor in the middle of the AIDS crisis. Porter's Pray emcees these affairs—throwing out shade and reading like it was his birthright—but also acts as a house father, all while dealing with his own HIV positive status.

The show instantly catapulted Porter to a new type of fame that, frankly, was a long time coming. He's been open about his struggle to get recognized in theater and Hollywood, refusing to play the stereotypes that were offered to him. "The world has caught up with me, and I'm a living witness that dreams do come true, even if they aren't the ones you start out with," he wrote in an essay for the *New York Times*.

When Porter speaks to the press, it often feels like he's schooling the reporters and readers—teaching people how to be kinder and more aware. His aphorisms have landed him BuzzFeed posts like "You're Not Living Your Best Life 'Til You've Heard Billy Porter's 7 Rules To Live By." But Porter is never offering trite self-help. He's just real. In an interview with *Esquire*, he declared, "Save yourself, children. Get out and save yourself." If he's talking about *Pose*, he's often espousing the forgotten history of queer minorities in the midst of a plague, discussing what it means to be a survivor. He's issued searing indictments of an industry that tried to pigeonhole him until he found his own path. He has said, talking to the *Guardian*, that he wants to be "present for the younger generation, so I can help them." His words echo throughout the web, almost as loudly as his outfits.

And part of his mission involves stepping out wearing gowns and dresses. It's all part of a plan to change the world. "I want to flip the question of what it means to be a man," he told the *New York Times*. "This question of masculinity, this sort of microscope of heteronormative masculinity that we are very often held up to, especially as leading men, needs to be shattered. You know, it's toxic and I'm over it and I've lived it and I'm not doing it anymore." His outfits pay homage to the past. That Oscars look? A tribute to one of the legends of the balls, Hector Xtravaganza; that Tonys cape was made out of the *Kinky Boots* curtain after the show closed. It doesn't hurt that he looks amazing while doing all of this. Cheering Porter on is a multifaceted experience: As you're screaming for his incredible outfits, you're also screaming for someone who represents true achievement beyond Hollywood benchmarks.

Porter's performance on *Pose* has earned him one of the highest accolades in his field, making history in the process. When he won the Emmy in 2019, he became the first openly gay Black man to receive that honor. His work on the show earns him plaudits online, but his werk on carpets inspires reactions that are close to euphoria. Perhaps the reaction is best summed up in the look on Glenn Close's face when she saw him at the 2019 Oscars. The actress is agog, her mouth wide open, gazing upon his finery. It's incredibly relatable.

Porter is not just our Internet Boyfriend; he's also, basically, our idol, someone, who through everything he does, inspires us to be the better, stronger, more beautiful version of ourselves. On *Pose*, he's assumed the role of a zaddy for a younger dancer in a plotline that affirms his own desirability—as if there were any question about that. In his real life, Porter proves that sexy is not limited by gendered ideas of what men and women are supposed to wear: A man can put on a dress and look hot to both men and women. But it's not just the clothes. It's his words. Porter gives us lessons to live by every time he opens his mouth.

SEXY SUBJECT:

KEANU REEVES

PLACE OF ORIGIN: Beirut

NATURAL HABITAT: On the back of a motorcycle

ATTRIBUTES: Low voice, shaggy mane, an altruistic soul

Is an Internet Boyfriend born or made? There's no better case study than Keanu Reeves. Keanu has always been hot; Keanu has not always been an Internet Boyfriend.

What are your earliest memories of Keanu Reeves? Do you see a floppy-haired boy with a goofy smile splashed across his face in *Bill and Ted's Excellent Adventure*? Or a rain-soaked Johnny Utah giving a thumbs-up in *Point Break* with, yes, a goofy smile splashed across his face? When you think of baby Keanu, you probably think of something joyful and a little silly. That's because the role that made him a star, time-traveling stoner Ted "Theodore" Logan, also tainted him. For years it was hard to get the notion of Keanu as doof-bro out of your head. No matter what part he played, the insidious idea that he was just a brainless dude who could only say "whoa" followed him. It maybe has something to do with his seemingly eternally youthful beauty at that time. Or perhaps the fact that he was so good at playing the archetypal neophyte that his character in *The Matrix* was literally named "Neo." (In that movie he also said "whoa." Whoa.) He's always had devoted fans, but only recently did loving Keanu become a movement.

The truth is: Keanu has hidden depths. His career is insanely varied. A silly comedy in which he kidnaps Napoleon may have been his calling card, but he did independent films like *My Own Private Idaho* and period pieces like *Much Ado*

About Nothing before *Speed* and *The Matrix* made him an action star. He has long elicited effusive praise from his colleagues, who were eager to paint a picture of him as more layered than his reputation would suggest. Sandra Bullock once called him the "Little Keester" in an *Entertainment Weekly* interview while talking about how good of a listener he was; director Gus Van Sant remarked on how smart Keanu really is, while at the same time noting how good he was at acting dumb.

So when did Keanu start winning everyone over wholeheartedly? I'd pinpoint the moment as when some punks killed the puppy his dead wife gave him. Now, of course, no one actually killed Keanu's puppy. (Though, admittedly, his real life has been studded with tragedy.) Instead the pooch in question belonged to John Wick of the eponymous action franchise. But John Wick and Keanu share the same essence. John Wick is the full evolution of the "Sad Keanu" meme, which endeared him to the internet as a dude who was okay with just sitting on a bench and being in his feelings.

A quick detour for "Sad Keanu." One day, sometime around 2010, Keanu decided to sit on a park bench and eat a sandwich. That's just the kind of celebrity he is. No need for seclusion or a gourmet meal: just an outdoor space and grub that appears to be from a bodega. His countenance looked a little downcast, but that's possibly just how we all look when we're focusing on our food. Anyway, people loved it partially because of the puzzlingly existential look on his face and partially because it just seemed so aggressively normal for a very famous person. More photos kept cropping up in this vein: Keanu, outside, in his feelings. "Sad Keanu" set us down the path that landed us where we are today. "Sad Keanu" set the stage for John Wick.

Before John Wick, Keanu hadn't had a critical hit in a while. But Wick turned him into a phenomenon once again, fully introducing audiences to a new era of awesomeness. In the series of movies, he plays the world's most feared assassin who had given up his life of death for his one great love. But when she succumbs to disease and some jerks steal his car and murder his little beagle, he gets his stash of guns and goes on a rampage, seeking vengeance for his lost pooch. As John Wick, Keanu has lost his boyish charm. He never flashes that wide-eyed grin. His face is peppered with stubble. His long hair falls in front of his eyes.

Although the plots of the *John Wick*s are simple, there's something soulful about the *idea* of John Wick the character thanks to Keanu. John Wick has a strong moral code . . . just like we imagine Keanu Reeves does. John Wick would protect you . . . just like we imagine Keanu Reeves would. John Wick is incredibly devoted . . . just like we imagine Keanu Reeves is.

It helps that Keanu lives his life in such a way that allows us to believe he's just as wonderful as we think he is. He gives up his seat for women on the subway, which he takes in lieu of private cars. He helps an entire plane of people get to their destination when an emergency landing leaves them stranded. He runs an imprint for avant-garde books with supercool visual artist Alexandra Grant, who is also his longtime girlfriend. When Stephen Colbert asks him what happens when we die, he says: "I know the ones who love us will miss us." That's Keanu for you: Thinking of others before himself even when considering life's biggest questions.

Yes, it's Keanu's slightly-but-not-too-grizzled looks that make him zaddy, as well as the fact that he wears a suit better than maybe anyone else in the world while displaying martial arts skills that would put Olympic athletes to shame. But it's also the fact that Keanu just seems like the type of guy who would go out of his way to lend a hand. He would stop whatever he was doing for you, but it would be no big deal. Keanu goes where the wind takes him, and the wind takes him to altruism.

Imagine: One day you'll need a lift and suddenly a man will ride up on a motorcycle. His voice will be low and his mane shaggy. He'll say, "Need a ride?" You'll reply, "Yes." Suddenly the helmet comes off and there is Keanu. Whoa.

SEXY SUBJECT:

PAUL RUDD

PLACE OF ORIGIN: Kansas by way of New Jersey

NATURAL HABITAT: Watching a Chiefs game

ATTRIBUTES: Nice guy demeanor, ageless beauty

In a segment from *Billy on the Street*—a pop culture-heavy comedy game show set on the sidewalks of New York—host Billy Eichner poses a question to a passerby: "Who would you rather have sex with Chris Evans or Paul Rudd?" The woman is unfazed. She answers "Rudd" without even considering. Now, to raise the stakes, Eichner has both Evans and Rudd beside him, but even upon realizing that they were present, the lady has no regrets. Rudd was Josh in *Clueless* and therefore everything she said stands. That's the thing about Paul Rudd: He was an Internet Boyfriend before everyone even had access to the internet. And he hasn't aged a goddamn day since.

Rudd's seemingly eternally pleasant looks are a big reason the internet has fixated him. Whereas other stars have had to recalibrate their careers to fit their changing appearances, Paul Rudd has basically always been the *same* guy because he appears to have made some sort of Dorian Gray–like deal with the devil to maintain a preternaturally youthful visage. But, it's actually unfair to say that Rudd has never aged. He has. He's just gotten better looking as he's gotten older. Somehow, the man has defied the natural order of things. So while a quiz like Vulture's "Can You Tell Which Paul Rudd Is Older?" remains one of the most challenging tests there is, it's just because Paul Rudd himself is playing tricks with your mind. Rudd's agelessness is his superpower, but it's not his only virtue.

Just like that passerby explained to Eichner, the root of the love for Rudd might go all the way back to Amy Heckerling's 1995 teen comedy *Clueless*. In the movie, Rudd plays Josh, the heroine Cher Horowitz's grungy ex-stepbrother who hangs around her Beverly Hills mansion when not going to his college classes. He teases her for her mall-rat proclivities, and she teases him for his goatee buried in a copy of Nietzsche. (She also totally owns his pretentious friend by remembering *Hamlet* thanks to the Mel Gibson movie.) But at the end of the day, Cher realizes she's "majorly, totally, butt-crazy in love with Josh," and the movie ends with them kissing. It's a wish fulfillment fantasy that's also just a tad incest-y. Yeah, we are working out some complicated feelings here.

It also explains why we have spent all these years obsessing over Paul Rudd. He's somehow both a big brother figure and a boyfriend. And, yes, it's a little weird, but you have to just roll with it. He's the dude who teases you, but it never crosses over from endearing to annoying. For example: He's been playing the same joke on Conan O'Brien for fifteen years now, showing a horrendous scene involving a goofy-looking alien and a kid in a wheelchair falling off a cliff from the *E.T.* rip-off *Mac and Me* instead of a clip from whatever he's promoting. Or there's the more recent revelation during his appearance on the hot wing–themed web talk show "Hot Ones" that he takes photos of fellow celebrities in such a manner that it looks like they are framed by a butt. (These famous people are not actually framed by butts, they are framed by Rudd's fingers made to look like butts and balls and other nasty bits.) That appearance also inspired yet another Rudd meme in which he cheerily ruminates on his good fortune. "Look at us," he tells the host, Sean Evans. "Hey, look at us?" Evans responds: "Who woulda thought?" Rudd volleys back, cheerfully: "Not me."

Rudd's whole life has been defined by these little contradictions. He was brought up in Kansas, but his parents hail from England. In another universe, perhaps he would have become a Benedict Cumberbatch type, known best for his Shakespearean chops. (Not that he hasn't done Shakespeare. He has. Multiple times. Who can forget when he made us reconsider our allegiance to a young Leonardo DiCaprio as Paris in Baz Luhrmann's *Romeo + Juliet*?) *Clueless* too offers a road not traveled for Rudd. He could have spent a career playing the romantic lead. Instead, he went weird.

He fell in with the alt-comedy crowd that made the bizarro classic *Wet Hot American Summer*, playing a warped idea of the hot guy. If you want to know the pinnacle of comedy, it's Rudd, in tight jeans, throwing a fit about having to put away his plate in the cafeteria. Three years later, Judd Apatow put him in *Anchorman: The Legend of Ron Burgundy* as bloviating newscaster Brian Fantana, who believes he can seduce ladies with a rancid cologne known as "Sex Panther." The association with Apatow gave Rudd a new life as a movie star, one that found him frequently playing the second banana. His role in *The 40-Year-Old Virgin* perhaps perfectly encapsulates this. He's a shaggy-haired loser, who works with Steve Carell's titular innocent nerd. Sure, Rudd's character isn't a virgin, but he *is* a desperate sad sack, longing to get back together with a girl who has definitely moved on. His run of Apatovian heroes mix that traditional Rudd appeal with a streak of despair. Men like Pete in *Knocked Up* and *This Is 40* are cheerful enough on the outside, but are masking wells of disappointment. Even when he ended up—like so many actors do nowadays—in a Marvel movie, he nabbed arguably the oddest comic book character ever to have his own franchise: Ant-Man.

Whether an actor can be both funny and hot has been the subject of many intentionally silly debates online, and Rudd often lands on the funny rather than hot side of the equation. (I once argued *against* the idea of Rudd being primarily hot. I admit now that I was wrong.) The very idea of Ant-Man is funny. He's a man . . . who turns into . . . an ant. But this is a superhero in the MCU, after all. Hotness would be required, and Rudd stepped up to the task, getting ripped in the process, without losing his perfect timing. Yes, somehow Rudd managed to make a movie about a former career criminal who gains the ability to shrink down to the size of teeny little bug work. That's the thing about this guy: Even though he appears to be a perfect subject of a human, he is simultaneously the perpetual underdog. And you can't help but root for an underdog. Or a dude who make butts out of his fingers. Who would have thought?

KUMAIL NANJIANI

December 16, 2019, was an auspicious day. It was the day that Kumail Nanjiani posted his first beefcake photo on Instagram. Before that photo was unleashed on the web, Nanjiani was certainly not known for his physique, but he was well on the way to Internet Boyfriend status even without a six pack. (Though it's not like the six pack hurts his cause.)

The Pakistani-born comedian first became known to most for playing software engineer Dinesh on *Silicon Valley*. Now, Dinesh, alas, is not boyfriend material. Sure, he's got Nanjiani's impressive jawline, but, like most of the characters on the HBO comedy, Dinesh sort of sucks. He's a desperate jerk with delusions of grandeur who is the butt of jokes. He's a funny desperate jerk with delusions of grandeur who is the butt of jokes, but that kind of guy nonetheless. Dinesh once got his girlfriend arrested by the FBI. You would not want to date Dinesh.

So we don't love Nanjiani because of his most famous character. Rather, Nanjiani's crush potential skyrocketed when he started getting personal. We know for a fact that he is an amazing real-life partner, which is why he makes a great Internet Boyfriend as well. He and his wife Emily V. Gordon canonized their love story—arguably one of the greatest of all time—in 2017's *The Big Sick*. The movie, which also starred Nanjiani, tells the story of how he and Gordon met and fell for each other all before she became gravely ill and was put in a medically induced coma. Instead of abandoning the relationship—which already had a lot to overcome given Nanjiani's family's disapproval and desire to arrange a marriage for him—he waited for her.

We here in Internet Boyfriend Land love a rom-com, and *The Big Sick* is one of the reasons the genre started to undergo a renaissance at the end of the 2010s. And while the film was great, the actual people it was about seemed even better. Nanjiani gets permanent points for a) having a cool wife and b) being absolutely, totally in love with his cool wife.

But, okay, back to the bod. Nanjiani is certainly not the first comedian to get ripped to play a superhero. Chris Pratt initiated the trend when he ditched his Andy Dwyer belly for Star-Lord's defined pecs. Internet Boyfriend Paul Rudd buffed up for *Ant-Man*. But Nanjiani is maybe the first to do so in an incredibly honest, upfront way when he got jacked to star in the Marvel movie *The Eternals*. When he posted that glistening image, he wrote: "I never thought I'd be one of those people who would post a thirsty shirtless, but I've worked way too hard for way too long so here we are. You either die a hero, or you live long enough to see yourself become the villain." He also admitted that he was only able to change thanks to trainers and nutritionists, all of which were backed by a huge corporation—you know, Disney. That's a crucial addition to his not-so-humblebrag: No, you cannot look this way without a lot of money and a lot of time.

But getting really, really, traditionally hot doesn't seem to have changed Kumail's personality at all. He's enjoying his new look, but recognizes how silly it all is, including the fact that his dad made socks with those pictures on them. He's used this new asset to cosplay his favorite movies like *Die Hard* and *American Psycho*. And he and Emily are still as cute as ever, even doing a podcast for charity called "Staying In" in the midst of the coronavirus crisis. That fateful Instagram post may have made us perk up, but don't be mistaken: Kumail Nanjiani was always going to be an Internet Boyfriend.

SEXY SUBJECT:

HARRY STYLES

PLACE OF ORIGIN: Worcestershire, England

NATURAL HABITAT: A recording studio

ATTRIBUTES: Blouses, wide trousers, impish grin

It's virtually impossible to dig into the history of celebrity crushes without discussing boy bands. Stemming back to the days of the Beatles, boy bands have been crush incubators, known as much for their music as for their ability to pose on posters that hang on teenage bedroom walls. While the modern idea of boy bands existed before the '90s, the decade turned boy bands into an industry with the likes of Backstreet Boys and NSYNC eliciting mobs of screaming fans. For the first decade of the 2000s—after the leftovers from the '90s faded from relevance—it seemed like the era of the boy band was over. And then a couple of lads from England—and one from Ireland—came along.

One Direction was not born organically. Each member of the fivesome auditioned for *The X Factor* as a solo act. Then Simon Cowell had a genius idea: Individually, they would probably generate some amount of buzz. Together, they would be unstoppable. Cowell was right. One Direction mania jumped across the pond and initiated a new era of boy band worship. This group was different from its '90s predecessors. They were shaggy and didn't really dance. But their fans were also different. These were kids raised by the internet, and they expressed their love for Harry Styles, Louis Tomlinson, Zayn Malik, Liam Payne, and Niall Horan as such. Stanning for One Direction involved slash fiction and Tumblr.

But when the time came, One Direction faced an age-old boy band question: What happens when they break up? Who becomes famous? For years, the pinnacle of post–boy band success had always been Justin Timberlake, crying a river all over the radio. (He also found controversy along the way. No, we will never forgive him for throwing Janet Jackson under the bus at the Super Bowl.) But who becomes the Joey Fatone? One thing was always certain: Harry Styles was a goddamn star. Styles had always been the likeliest candidate for post–One D fame. He was the most rambunctious of the group, as at home palling around on talk shows as he was crooning on the stage.

Still, no one could have predicted what he was about to unleash. Styles, on his own, somehow surpassed the promise of his early career. The individual that emerged was like the love child of David Bowie and Stevie Nicks, all flowing blouses, wide-legged pants, and funky vibes. He occupies a space in between the masculine and the feminine and is an ally without being obnoxious about it.

When he left the womb of One Direction, his goal was to write his own material. The sound that emerged was not Timberlake's white boy soul or the radio-ready pop of his bandmate Zayn Malik. Instead, it was a throwback hybrid of folk rock and pop—not a complete copy of an era that was not his own, but more indebted to his predecessors than his contemporaries.

The narrative around Harry Styles is that he is a Very Good Boy. It starts with his devotion to his mother, with whom he is reportedly very close. More proof of his sweetheart status can be found in the story about how he ended up being a polite houseguest to his friend *The Late Late Show with James Corden* producer Ben Winston for twenty months. As his star was rising in One Direction, he was crashing with an Orthodox Jewish family. "That period of time, he was living with us in the most mundane suburban situation," Winston once explained. "No one ever found out, really. Even when we went out for a meal, it's such a sweet family neighborhood, no one dreamed it was actually him. But he made our house a home. And when he moved out, we were gutted."

It's anecdotes like this—revealed in the singer's first *Rolling Stone* cover story, written by none other than *Almost Famous* director Cameron Crowe—that frame Styles as a superstar who is relatively down to earth, a *nice* person who cares about being good to those around him. I mean, one of the songs on his recent album *Fine Line* is titled "Treat People with Kindness." Styles once said: "There are others. People who are successful, and still nice. It's when you meet the people who are successful and aren't nice, you think: What's yer excuse? Cos I've met the other sort."

Styles gives off the impression that if you were to hang out with him you'd probably have a pretty pleasant and slightly wild time. Profiles of Styles tend to include stories about parties on beaches where nudity or clothes swapping is involved. He's spoken about how doing mushrooms influenced his latest record, *Fine Line*, and once led him to bite off the tip of his tongue. But even though that detail sounds like it might belong in an outtake from a seedier history of rock 'n' roll—think: Mötley Crüe—it's bizarrely wholesome coming from Styles, who has gone out of his way to promote a message of inclusion.

Though he's publicly only been linked to women, he's never exactly declared himself straight, either, and has alluded to bisexuality in his lyrics. One time, he declared, "We're all a little bit gay, aren't we?" Regardless of how he himself identifies, he's made it a mission to promote a safe-for-all environment at his shows. On one tour stop, he took note of a girl in the crowd's sign which declared she was going to come out to her parents because of him. He asked her mom's name, quieted the room, and shouted, "Tina, she's gay," triumphantly. It's an especially welcome development for someone whose early celebrity was defined by slash fiction with which some of his bandmates were openly uncomfortable.

His style started to evolve with his own fluidity as well. He took to wearing ruffles and low-cut shirts with wide-legged trousers. The effect was circus ringmaster mixed with '70s Laurel Canyon chic. There's a cheekiness to the look, evidenced by photo shoots in which he affects like he just told a dirty joke. He has said he dresses this way not because he's trying to allude to anything, just because he thinks it looks cool. And, the thing is, it does.

Harry Styles may have been made in the confines of the boy band universe, but when he struck out on his own, his message became freedom. He makes the music he wants, wears the clothes he wants, and encourages everyone around him to love who they want—even if that's just Harry Styles.

K-POP

One Direction is the past of boy bands. K-pop is its present and future. I'm admittedly a newbie to the world, and there are those out there who have spent years and years living and breathing and stanning it. K-pop's been around since the 1990s, but its global profile has never been higher. In 2019, BTS was declared the biggest band in the world. That's how high. And while K-pop groups can be massive in size, that doesn't mean that fans still don't isolate certain members to obsess over like BTS's RM, Suga, and Jimin. K-pop stans can also be mobilized for good. They have used their savvy understanding of social media to fight against police brutality and white supremacy. When BTS donated $1 million dollars to Black Lives Matter, their Army matched it.

But BTS is just an entry point. There are plenty of groups to stan: Consider Monsta X or EXO or NCT 127.

SEXY SUBJECT:

STANLEY TUCCI

PLACE OF ORIGIN: Peekskill, New York

NATURAL HABITAT: A big kitchen in an Italian villa

ATTRIBUTES: Shapely bald head, big glasses, burly arms deep in a bowl of pasta

When did you realize Stanley Tucci was hot? Was it when he and Tony Shalhoub built the pasta cake known as a Timpano in *Big Night*? Or was it when he was Emma Stone's understanding father in *Easy A* wearing those tight t-shirts? Maybe it was when he played the supportive husband to Meryl Streep's Julia Child in *Julie & Julia*. Or did you figure out you had a weird thing for Caesar Flickerman in *The Hunger Games*? (No judgment if you did. This is a safe space.)

The thing is: It's a well-established fact that Tucci is hot. His hotness has been immortalized on novelty t-shirts like the one that reads "I Like My Coffee Like Stanley Tucci . . . Hot" and in BuzzFeed posts like "Stanley Tucci Is Insanely Hot In 'Easy A' And We Need To Talk About It." Vulture once contributed to the Tucci love in the form of the essay "Stanley Tucci's 12 Most Adorable Movie Roles."

Stanley Tucci is an interesting case in the realm of Internet Boyfriends. He is, after all, traditionally handsome, but he has not made his career on being traditionally handsome. He's one of Hollywood's preeminent character actors, best known for playing sidekicks and villains rather than romantic leads. That's perhaps what makes his stealth run as an Internet Boyfriend so surprising.

Still, Tucci represents a whole subset of Internet Boyfriends who are not your typical heartthrobs. With the rise of daddy and zaddy culture, offbeat types like the Tooch are finally being appreciated the way they should be. Some other examples? Tucci's costar in *Big Night*, Tony Shalhoub, who finally began to get sex symbol status when he played the stern father on *The Marvelous Mrs. Maisel*. Go figure. Or there's Kyle McLachlan who generated renewed devotion taking on three weirdos in *Twin Peaks: The Return* and posting on his endearing social media accounts about his wine. Sam Neill won us over with his Twitter content about his farm and animals named after other celebrities. What about Andy Garcia? He spent the summer of 2018 wooing female film legends like Diane Keaton and Cher and was crowned a silver fox zaddy.

But for now we're focusing on Stanley Tucci. There are plenty of reasons why Tucci evolved into an obsession. It could be his well-calibrated performances, like the exacting editor Nigel in *The Devil Wears Prada*. Or it could be the discovery of a Levi's ad he made in the 1980s in which he appears all muscled up in a tank top. But I'd argue that the number one way that Tucci wormed his way into each one of our hearts is through our stomachs.

Stanley Tucci is a big Italian feast of a human being. The ideal version of Tucci involves his sleeves rolled up, his forearms covered in dough, and his knuckles deep in a bed of focaccia. Of course, this has a lot to do with his involvement in one of the greatest food films of all time. After years as a steadily working actor, he made his directorial debut in 1996 with the aforementioned *Big Night*. He plays one of two Italian immigrant brothers who are struggling to keep their restaurant afloat in 1950s New Jersey. He's not the chef—that would be Shalhoub—but the beauty of watching him tap on the pasta cake known as a Timpano or silently cook eggs would create fantasies for years to come. In *Julie & Julia* he savors food with such relish he creates the image of the ideal man with whom to share some boeuf bourguignon. (Read the name of that dish in a Julia Child accent if you so wish.)

This stems into his personal life too. Tucci has coauthored multiple cookbooks featuring homey Italian recipes alongside other members of his family. If you get one, and let Tucci teach you how to make gnocchi and linguine with clam sauce, you get to imagine you've invited him into your home. Or you could simulate that a little more literally by watching his CNN travel show: *Stanley Tucci: Searching for Italy*.

Tucci has made food part of his own love story as well. He was a widower—his first wife died of cancer—when he met his current spouse, Felicity Blunt, bonding at the wedding of her sister, his *Devil Wears Prada* costar Emily. He describes their courtship as food-centric. They plucked feathers off pheasants and roasted a twenty-six-pound suckling pig together. It's desire mixed with a hint of gluttony, and it's yummy.

Tucci went viral during the coronavirus pandemic by demonstrating how to make a Negroni in a snug t-shirt, with a sultry voice. At the end of the video, clearly filmed by Felicity, he asks if she wants the drink then teasingly says, "That will never happen." It's a dreamy glimpse into their relationship.

Even when the sight of him is not conjuring the smell of sweet and spicy Bolognese, Tucci is almost always a welcome sight on-screen. He works constantly, and even when the projects are not, let's just say, the pinnacle of creative endeavors, he brings a significant amount of joy. (See, for instance, his multiple appearances in various *Transformers* movies.) Whenever Tucci shows up, you know you're in for a little bit of flash and often a whole lot of warmth. In his best roles, he emits a comforting aura that makes you just want to curl up with him and a big bowl of spaghetti.

The curse of the character actor is to mostly go underappreciated while the bigger stars hog the spotlight. But Tucci has created such a cult of his own that there was a *Saturday Night Live* sketch—a parody of the song "Gucci Gang"—inspired by love for the Tooch. It was called "Tucci Gang." If being part of the Tucci Gang means eating well and loving Stanley Tucci, well, sign us up.

INTERNET BOYFRIENDS EMERITUS

Let's shout out the men who will never lose their luster.

BRAD PITT: After a banner awards run in 2020, Brad Pitt reminded us that he will always and forever be a heartthrob.

BRUCE SPRINGSTEEN: Young Bruce Springsteen is good. Old Bruce Springsteen is good. Bruce Springsteen is good.

ANTONIO BANDERAS: From Almodóvar and the art house to Zorro, Banderas is zaddy.

PRINCE: Dearly beloved, we are gathered here today to pay tribute to a man of many names who will always bring the funk to our hearts.

COLIN FIRTH AND HUGH GRANT: The *Bridget Jones* and *Love Actually* guys just keep getting better with age.

TONY LEUNG: A legend of Hong Kong cinema. Also gorgeous.

LEONARDO DICAPRIO (CIRCA 1997): Look, Leo may have evolved. But our hearts will forever go on for that guy on that boat.

HUMPHREY BOGART: We know how to whistle, and we will whistle for Bogie any day.

PAUL NEWMAN AND ROBERT REDFORD: An eternal pair.

THE INTERNET BOYFRIENDS

♥

THE

INTERNET

GIRLFRIENDS

♥

SEXY SUBJECT:

CARDI B

PLACE OF ORIGIN: The Bronx

NATURAL HABITAT: The Bronx, obviously

ATTRIBUTES: Bloody shoes, great nails, hilarious observations

Is there anything better than just listening to Cardi B talk? Something about hearing her go on about whatever is somehow the most wonderful feeling in the world. It's like taking a shot of tequila, straight no chaser. You get the rush and then are overcome by an inexplicable calm. This self-professed "regular degular shmegular girl" from the Bronx, who is now anything but a regular degular shmegular girl, won us all over just by speaking her mind. The worldwide sensation that is Cardi B was born on the internet. Specifically, she was born on Instagram where, even before she had number one hits, she would hold court about her day-to-day activities.

By now, if you have a vague interest in pop culture, you probably know how the woman formerly known as Belcalis Almanzar got to where she is. (In a 2016 tweet she explained how to pronounce "Belcalis Almanzar" and then went on, "Nobody in the fucking world got my name. So I like it. If you don't like it, I don't give a fuck, suck my dick with your basic ass name.")

She grew up in the Bronx. She went to an arts-focused high school and then enrolled in community college. Just before she was fired from her job at a grocery store, her manager suggested she try stripping at a club nearby. Soon came social media stardom largely via Instagram where she would post unvarnished screeds. That landed her on VH1's reality show

Love & Hip Hop New York. In a post declaring her the "break-out star" of the show, Jezebel's Clover Hope perfectly summed up her appeal: "Besides being loud, strange, funny and self-aware—all the right reality ingredients—she's debatably real in a world that's blatantly fabricated, which makes her a welcome face to fans thirsting for honest characters." It's amusing that as recently as 2016 we were discussing Cardi just in terms of reality TV stardom. Oh how soon that would change.

Then in 2017 she released "Bodak Yellow," a track that stomped on your neck with its bloody shoes and made you completely helpless. With "Bodak Yellow," Cardi announced her intentions with force: "I don't dance now, I make money moves." It was such a strong statement of intent there was no question she was going global. And all the while she maintained her habits of talking straight to her fans. So if we're talking about celebrity crushes, especially ones who have been shaped by the internet, we have to talk about Cardi.

Can we count the reasons we love Cardi? Probably not, they are multitude. But one of the reasons? She's just so funny. Take, for instance, a video she posted in September 2019. Cardi, in full hair and makeup, goes on a rant about how angry she gets when a woman acts fake when she has a new man in her life. She seems *mad.* Just before she's done, she sits back and changes her tone. "But I don't got friends like that so

I can't relate," she says, sweetly. She executes this punch line with perfect comic timing. Cardi B knows she's funny, and she milks it whenever she can. She punctuates her speech with her now signature purr of "Okurrrr" or the crafty cackle she appends to some of her wisdom.

It's not that fame hasn't changed Cardi at all. It has. It changes everyone, and she's been up front about the way her life has morphed, even cosmetically. At the same time, she's still appearing without makeup or washing her face on Twitter and still posting videos like the one I've just described.

Cardi is not immune to controversy. Her relationship with her husband and father of her child, Migos rapper Offset, has been one sticking point in particular. Offset cheated, and Cardi very publicly took him back. She also is battling charges stemming from a fight at a strip club, which her accusers say she orchestrated to get back at a woman who had sex with Offset. She's treated each court appearance as an opportunity for high fashion, strutting in perfectly tailored suits and fur.

The chaos of her personal life seemed to largely fade away after she had her child Kulture. Her feeds were still raucous, but also devoted to the day-to-day of mothering. The film director Greta Gerwig praised Cardi's pregnancy content in an interview with *Vogue*, explaining that it gave her comfort during her own pregnancy. "She'd do videos about how her hair looked better, but then she was mad because she had terrible heartburn," Gerwig said. "Everything. I would eat it up. I've just been very moved by women who've claimed all of it."

Cardi's outspokenness has also recently translated to political activism that pulls absolutely no punches. She's a scholar of history and told *GQ* she's "obsessed with presidents." Her activist statements seem to come from a place of real anger and frustration, like when she told *Vogue*: "It's like, why is this such a successful country and we don't have Medicare for everyone? It's like, how are people gonna work if they're sick? People gonna fucking be paying forever." It's all in keeping with the Cardi ethos. When she's pissed off, she's not shy about it. At times it gets her into trouble, but that's the cost of being as free with your emotions as Cardi is.

When other celebrities are crafting carefully orchestrated statements, Cardi is just simply popping off. It's not that her image isn't carefully crafted; it's that it's entirely crafted on her own terms. My (not Internet) boyfriend's oft-repeated adage is that the only good thing about the Trump era is Cardi B. He's not wrong. There are a lot of people yelling on the internet these days: Cardi B's voice is the only one of those that provides any sort of solace.

SEXY SUBJECT:

LAURA DERN

PLACE OF ORIGIN: Los Angeles

NATURAL HABITAT: The Chateau Marmont with David Lynch

ATTRIBUTES: Gorgeous blonde hair, great at screaming

There is almost nothing more cathartic than looking at a GIF of Laura Dern yelling or crying. Dern yelling in *Big Little Lies* against a beautiful ocean backdrop wearing designer finery, her body hunching over the weight of her scream. Or then again you can have Dern, face mascara coated, wailing on a toilet in *Enlightened*. That doesn't suit your mood? What about Dern's contorted visage in *Blue Velvet*?

Even out of context, a Laura Dern performance can provide a sense of glorious relief. She can encapsulate all your sorrow or all your rage with just a movement or a gesture. Dern is our Internet Girlfriend, but she is also our avatar for every emotion we could possibly want to feel. Dern can be anything you want her to be: The expression of your agony or the motherly figure just telling you it's all going to be okay. Even though we don't know her personally, it just feels like Dern is there for us.

Dern also didn't earn this level of adoration until later in life, despite the fact that she has basically grown up on-screen. A perfect storm of great career decisions, coupled with an adept use of social media, threw Dern back into public consciousness in an unprecedented way. This isn't to say that Laura Dern hasn't *always* been amazing. To know Dern is to love her entire career, but as she has gotten older, she started to occupy a different space. Laura Dern is no longer a virtuosic upstart. Instead, she's who we want to be when we grow up—passion and anger included. (And if we could get the wardrobe she wears as Renata for ourselves, that wouldn't be so bad either.)

The daughter of screen legends Diane Ladd and Bruce Dern, Dern got started in the business almost as soon as she could. She even got emancipated from her parents when she was a teen—not to get away from them, but because she wanted to make her own professional decisions.

Her talents were recognized by directors like David Lynch, the deeply weird auteur who became her longtime collaborator, and the acerbic Alexander Payne. She could somehow be everything at once: Lynch's twisted idea of the girl next door in *Blue Velvet* or an addict caught in the midst of a political maelstrom in Payne's *Citizen Ruth*. As Ellie Sattler in *Jurassic Park* she captured true wonder, while fending off a pack of hunting raptors. (She also made khaki shorts and an oversize pink button-down tied at the waist a major fashion statement.)

"Brave" is often used in a trite way when it comes to acting, but Dern's choices have always been just that. When there was still a potent stigma around coming out, she played the woman who precipitates Ellen DeGeneres's on the comedian's eponymous sitcom. She acts with a kind of abandon that is almost always exhilarating.

The point is: Laura Dern has deserved a cultlike devotion. Except the Church of Dern only started gathering followers in earnest in the last couple of years. The first stirrings of the Dernaissance happened with *Enlightened,* the brilliant but, at the time, underrated HBO show in which she was Amy Jellicoe, whose breakdown evolves into a do-gooder ethos and corporate sabotage. Still, recruitment started in earnest with *Big Little Lies.*

The HBO drama was essentially designed to be a media sensation, and Dern wasn't even its biggest star. When the show started, Reese Witherspoon's Madeline Martha Mackenzie was the most internet-friendly character, lobbing bon mots about her petty grievances. Nicole Kidman, meanwhile, was giving a heartbreaking performance as a woman in the middle of an abusive relationship. But it was Dern, as the tightly wound businesswoman Renata, that clicked more than anyone else. Renata wore power suits and was fiercely defensive of her ridiculously named child Amabella. Just about everything Dern did as Renata was easily turned into a meme. The same year, she strode into *Twin Peaks: The Return* in a white-blonde wig and a miniskirt effortlessly chain-smoking. Reuniting with Lynch, she tossed out insults like "Fuck you, Tammy," with a chilly finesse. More memes came. The roles could not be more different. One is an overly excitable Monterey mom and tycoon; another is a mystical being in the body of a fabulously dressed secretary.

It seemed like everyone was finally realizing that Laura Dern is a treasure. It helped that Dern, as a person, also gives the impression that she's, well, the greatest. Her Instagram account is just a bevy of warmth, whether that means fooling around with her famous friends or providing snapshots into her daily routines, be they glam sessions for awards shows or more mundane activities.

If she does something a little weird, she leans into it. Take the odd moment when a reporter asked her about Baby Yoda, and she replied that she had seen the character in the *Star Wars* show *The Mandalorian* at an NBA game. It was a strange answer that made no sense, but instead of explaining herself further, she just leaned into it, making seeing Baby Yoda at NBA games her thing, sort of. She somehow mixes a go-for-broke dorkiness—see the TikTok she made dancing with her daughter—with a perpetual state of aspirational iconoclasm.

Of course, her day-to-day activities seem blessed in just the most awesome way possible. She gets fried chicken every Sunday night at the Chateau Marmont with David Lynch, after all. She's had a standing Christmas Eve morning date with Courteney Cox for fourteen years now. And yet she gives the impression that she's also somehow down to earth. It's that motherly quality she is so good at conveying when she's in movies like *Wild* or *Little Women.* She comes off as a person who genuinely wants to hear your problems and would probably give damn good advice.

Dern represents everything that womanhood should be: sexy, pissed off, caring, and a total hoot. She screams, and we sometimes scream along.

SEXY SUBJECT:

JANELLE MONÁE

PLACE OF ORIGIN: Kansas City, Kansas

NATURAL HABITAT: Wondaland

ATTRIBUTES: Former android prone to wearing pussy pants

To talk about the internet's love story with Janelle Monáe, you have to talk about the pussy pants. By the time Monáe showed up in the video for her song "Pynk" wearing Georgia O'Keeffe-evoking pants that definitely resembled a certain bit of female anatomy, she had already become one of the web's most beloved modern celebrities. But the pants put her into the pantheon. The trousers, which essentially turned her legs into floral labia, were one of the most gloriously ostentatious displays of feminine power anyone had seen from a mainstream celebrity. They were beyond suggestive, they just came out and said what they meant—and what they meant was a beautiful declaration of queer female energy.

The vagina trousers were no onetime thing: Monáe's vibe had been trending in this direction for a while, growing her already substantial fan base and making her a do-no-wrong internet goddess. As she ramped up for the release of her 2018 album *Dirty Computer*, every move she made brought more women and men into her futurist coven. In the "Make Me Feel" video, she brought us into a funky club and somehow channeled Prince, David Bowie, and Robert Palmer all at once. In "Django Jane" she rapped, "Let the vagina have a monologue."

From the moment Monáe showed up on the scene, she was a critical success, but she also, intentionally, remained aloof.

We, as a culture, like our Internet Boyfriends and Girlfriends to reveal themselves. We like to feel like we *know* them, and for years that was not part of Monáe's aesthetic. She actively avoided that by deeming herself an android. On her first albums she played the part of Cindi Mayweather, a robot who fell in love with a human. When asked about her love life, she would say, "I only date androids." Creating Cindi was both a promotional strategy and a defense mechanism. Monáe didn't easily fit into the boxes that the media sets out for Black female artists, so she created a sci-fi vision in which she did fit. But that also, intentionally, set fans at arm's length.

Around 2016, she started revealing more of herself, largely thanks to cinema. She appeared in Barry Jenkins's Oscar-winning *Moonlight*, unadorned, playing the loving girlfriend of Internet Boyfriend Mahershala Ali's Juan. Even Jenkins himself was surprised to see Monáe out of character when he first Skyped with her for the role. He told the *New York Times*: "I wanted to call her Auntie. I was used to the pompadour, and this larger-than-life entity, the outer-space person that I'd seen live in Oakland with Erykah Badu, and I had to reconcile that person with this person before me." That same year she also starred in *Hidden Figures*, a historical drama about the Black women who were instrumental in the early days of NASA.

As an actor, Monáe had a naturalism she had purposefully rarely displayed before. Both the films were up for major trophies when awards season rolled around the following winter, and Monáe was the most welcome presence on the red carpet all season, popping in monochromatic tones that were somehow both retro and thoroughly modern all at once. To the Oscars she wore a gown with wide Elizabethan hips.

She transitioned from her acting acclaim back into music with the *Dirty Computer* era, which correlated with a renewed interest in her personal life: specifically her connection to one particular star. Monáe had long been publicly friends with Tessa Thompson, but people started to suspect that their friendship was perhaps more than that. It was a romantic relationship that the internet desperately wanted to be real.

You see, Thompson was also achieving Internet Girlfriend status during this period. A prolific actor who had been working since the mid-2000s, she gained a new level of fame thanks to a steady stream of roles in films like *Selma*, *Creed*, and *Thor: Ragnarok*. In that last movie, she played Valkyrie, a mythic warrior who slugs alcohol and sticks it to the blonde and beefy Asgardian hero. Thompson was vocal about how she intended to play Valkyrie as bisexual, even though Disney and Marvel didn't leave any explicit references to her character's sexuality in the final cut of the film. Thompson made her mark as an outspoken force with a pioneering sense of style, and for a time, it really seemed like she and Monáe were dating—a match made in internet heaven.

Just the very notion that that could be happening sent the rumor mill excitedly flying. Blogs analyzed the timeline of their relationship and their social media posts. (There were signs stemming back to even 2015.) And it's not like Monáe and Thompson did not display *some* form of mutual attraction. Thompson appeared as Monáe's love interest in the "Emotion Picture" that complemented *Dirty Computer*'s release. In "Pynk" she popped her head in between Monáe's legs clad in those vagina pants.

Both never officially confirmed the relationship, however. Monáe did eventually open up about her sexuality for a *Rolling Stone* piece. She defined herself as a "queer Black woman" and "someone who has been in relationships with both men and women," eventually concluding: "I consider myself to be a free-ass motherfucker." She said she's thought of herself as both bi and pansexual over the years. In January 2020, she tweeted "#IAmNonBinary," which was less a declaration of her own identity than a means of supporting others. Of course, both Monáe and Thompson are fully entitled to their privacy, but the hypothetical offered a power coupling beyond our wildest dreams.

And in the end, it didn't really matter whether they were "official" or not. Through Monáe's art, Monáe and Thompson were still offering queer people of color and allies something that felt entirely fresh. "I want young girls, young boys, nonbinary, gay, straight, queer people who are having a hard time dealing with their sexuality, dealing with feeling ostracized or bullied for just being their unique selves, to know that I see you," Monáe told *Rolling Stone* in describing her intended audience for the album.

Which brings me back to those pants. For Monáe, female sexuality, specifically female sexuality that's not straight or even necessarily cis, is not something to be reviled or hidden. It's something to be embraced and broadcast. If you're too squeamish to look and see its beauty, well, fuck you then.

SEXY SUBJECT:

KRISTEN STEWART

PLACE OF ORIGIN: Los Angeles

NATURAL HABITAT: A French film set

ATTRIBUTES: Worn-in t-shirt, motorcycle boots, heavy eyeliner, awesome DGAF attitude

I
t's difficult to pinpoint the moment Kristen Stewart went from being one of the most loathed celebrities on the planet to one of the most beloved. For so long Stewart was That Girl from *Twilight*. Then she was That Girl from *Twilight* Who Cheated On Her Hunky *Twilight* Boyfriend. But eventually all that slid away, and the true Stewart emerged, the Stewart with whom the internet fell in love. That Stewart was brash and unrepentantly herself. She gave incredible performances in independent films from female and foreign directors. She was an establishment-approved style icon that seemingly never compromised her personal taste for a brand's generic idea.

Stewart is a case study in growing up in the public eye, becoming exactly who you want to be, and saying "fuck you" to anyone who doesn't like that. And while she's still shaking off some of the assumptions that have followed her ever since she became a teen phenomenon, she's also transformed into something of the ultimate Internet Girlfriend—someone who is desirable in all senses of the word.

Before *Twilight* came along, Kristen Stewart was a promising child actress. Her career seemed to parallel that of Jodie Foster, her costar in David Fincher's *Panic Room*. But then she got the role of Bella Swan in the film adaptation of Stephenie Meyer's already immensely popular book series. The *Twilight* movies were melodramatic and campy, and taken incredibly seriously by their army of devoted fans. The fervent devotion was met by intense mockery, much of it aimed directly at Stewart, who, by the way, was totally aware of what kind of performance she was giving. She recently told Howard Stern she wanted to do a "cult-y, weird, indulgent . . . girly" role.

During the heyday of *Twilight* mania she was a young woman still figuring out her voice, who now admits she was suffering from debilitating anxiety. Her visible discomfort with media appearances made her the butt of jokes and subject of lists like "Kristen Stewart's 7 Most Awkward 'Twilight' Interviews." But it wasn't just *Twilight* that made her a target: It was her high-profile romance with costar Robert Pattinson, which was the subject of manic tabloid fascination. And then her life imploded. She was caught cheating with her *Snow White and the Huntsman* director.

Sometime around 2014 and 2015, something changed. The nervous, uncomfortable person she seemed to be through most of the *Twilight* saga was replaced by someone who was fully confident in who she is. She took on a defensive posture but didn't seem to want to shut the world out anymore. Instead, she started giving interviews that were brutally honest. She told *Marie Claire*: "Lately, I've been doing less of the [assumes whiny cry voice] 'I'm sooooo sorry.' And more of the [drops several octaves] 'No. Fuck. Jesus.'" (That phrase became such a mantra for me that I once put NFJ charms on a necklace for a friend.)

She appeared in lauded films like *Clouds of Sils Maria* and won the French equivalent of an Oscar for that. She cut her hair. She cursed as much as she wanted. She put the letters A-S-S on her basement wall. By early 2017, she came out, casually, in an *Saturday Night Live* monologue, explaining in a direct address and challenge to President Trump, who was weirdly obsessed with her relationship with RPattz, that she was "like so gay, dude." That same *SNL* she riffed on her new reputation as an arty queer icon in a sketch about Totino's pizza rolls wherein she awakens Vanessa Bayer's housewife from her life of robotic subservience. As silly as it may seem, the Totino's sketch captures the intoxicatingly rebellious energy of Kristen Stewart so well. It's easy to picture her breaking into your kitchen, embracing you, and opening you up to a whole universe of possibilities. And did we mention she's really funny? It's just in her nature to have the ability to turn an eye roll or an off-the-cuff remark into high art.

Her evolving style seemed to complement that. Now, no matter what Stewart wears she radiates a punk energy. Her neck is always hanging with chains. Her hair is cropped into a messy shag. Whether she's in heels or sneakers, she seems at ease in her own skin in a way that is aspirational. You just need to look at the way she moves to be in awe: The Rolling Stones video "Ride 'Em On Down" encapsulates this as she dances and drives in a crop top and jeans. She's our James Dean.

But the refreshing thing about Kristen Stewart is that even though she continually projects an air of DGAF cool, she clearly does GAF in a way that is truly, actually cool. When she talks about her work as an actress and the projects she chooses, she does so in a way that's brimming with unguarded passion. She's made multiple shorts and is planning to direct her own feature film about a woman coming to terms with her bisexuality. And as far back as 2009, she was challenging the idea that she had to act the part of someone who was always enthusiastic. "I am just trying not to say something totally un-genuine about something I love," she said in an interview with *Dazed*. "People have to try to understand that it's very weird for me to talk to people I don't know about something I care about so much."

Kristen Stewart never deserved the scorn she got. Even during the *Twilight* years her commitment and fundamental coolness were always there. The rest of the world just had to catch up. These days it's thrilling to see Stewart being loved for exactly who she is.

ROBERT PATTINSON

Since I've written at length about Kristen Stewart, it's only fair to acknowledge the Internet Boyfriend status of Robert Pattinson. Their paths are obviously interlinked. They both gained massive fame—and became the butt of jokes—thanks to *Twilight* and their relationship, then decided to swerve.

While Stewart has become an Internet Girlfriend thanks to her confidence and swagger, Pattinson has become an Internet Boyfriend because of his quietly oddball behavior. Pattinson comes off like a sort of sly jester—not a class clown exactly, but someone who gets a kick out of messing around. Pattinson became a star largely because people fell under the thrall of a twinkly vampire with unreal cheekbones, but he used that stardom to seemingly just entertain himself whether or not anyone else is particularly entertained. (Just FYI, Rob, we are entertained. Very entertained.) This has resulted in headlines like: "26 Times Robert Pattinson Was A Total Freakin' Weirdo" and "Robert Pattinson's Viral Moments, Ranked." That latter piece, in *GQ*, declares that "The indie icon is also the most wholesome Internet celebrity."

There is something pure about Pattinson's antics. Whereas with other people his behavior might read as insolence, with

Pattinson it comes off as weirdly endearing because there's a playfulness to it all. He seems both deadly serious while at the same time inviting us in on the joke. He's a little rascal whose hair you would just like to tousle.

So what are some of Pattinson's most engaging antics? Well, there are the years he spent ragging on *Twilight* while at the same time promoting *Twilight*, accurately pointing out that his character Edward Cullen would probably be an axe murderer. (It's worth noting that some of the behavior that now wins Pattinson praise is of the same ilk as the behavior that got Stewart trashed in the media. Double standards are incredibly real.)

In 2017, he wrote and starred in a video for *GQ* about his quest for a hot dog on the streets of New York City and his inability to act like a normal human being because of his celebrity. Pattinson, wearing a baseball hat and a jacket zipped all the way up, scurries around the city while his voice-over mutters borderline nonsense. At the end, he finally gets a hot dog, and triumphantly declares: "I knew I was just a normal human being. You can call me Rob. I eat hot dogs."

For more Pattinson oddness, consider this interview between him and Jennifer Lopez that lit Twitter on fire in 2019. At one point, Pattinson explains: "Something I was trying to find for years was to do a ballet movie. And then my agent was like, 'Why? Do you know how to ballet?' I'm like, 'No.'" Lopez, calling him "Bobby" as if they were old friends, presses him on why he's so interested in this ballet dream. "I think there's a ballerina inside me," he says. There's! A! Ballerina! Inside! Of! Him! The beauty of this statement has nothing to do with gender. It's the twenty-first century and men do ballet. Get with the program. No, the reason this is just so delightful is that Pattinson—a man who has no dance training and no real experience with dance—just wants nothing more than to do a movie about ballet.

Every career move Pattinson has made implies that he wants to challenge himself. He has worked with some of the greatest living filmmakers like Claire Denis and David Cronenberg. He went crazy in long johns in *The Lighthouse* and turned into a Queens dirtbag for *Good Time*. But while he's proving his muscle, it also seems like he's, well, having a lot of fun. We can only assume his choice to play Batman is for similar reasons. Robert Pattinson's mind is a kooky place, and we just want to live in it a little bit.

SEXY SUBJECT:

PHOEBE WALLER-BRIDGE

PLACE OF ORIGIN: London

NATURAL HABITAT: On an awards show stage

ATTRIBUTES: Birthmark underneath hairline, expressive eyes, being smarter than you are

It's well established that smoking, in actuality, isn't cool. Countless PSAs have shown us just how gross it makes your lungs, and the data is there to prove its link to cancer. However, smoking still *looks* really cool. You have to admit that, in the right context, it still conveys old-school glamour with a hint of rock and roll. Case in point: the photo of Phoebe Waller-Bridge celebrating her multiple Emmy wins in 2019 at the Chateau Marmont. The photo that went viral shows Waller-Bridge lounging in a poolside chair, flanked by her trophies. In one hand she has a vodka gimlet. In the other, the cigarette she's just taken a drag of, her gloriously pronounced chin lifted upward as she blows out. It's an image of a woman owning her triumph and enjoying it.

That whole night was a coronation of sorts for Waller-Bridge, who came away with three wins for her work on the second season of *Fleabag*, which had already been hailed as a masterpiece by critics. But up until the Emmys, Phoebe Waller-Bridge fandom still felt like something of a fun little secret held among those who were appropriately in the know. Even though she's now been christened by the establishment, she's just as crush-worthy as ever.

If you were in Britain, you might have had a passing sense of who Phoebe Waller-Bridge was before September 2016, when *Fleabag* launched on Amazon Prime, but for us

Americans that's when we largely got wind of her and her outsize talent. Even then, *Fleabag* was an underrated gem, the kind of show that TV critics would beg their friends to stream. The conversation would go something like: "It's from this virtually unknown British writer, and it's absolutely hilarious but devastating at the same time. It's also very horny in a fabulous and unhinged way. Yes, the character is just called 'Fleabag.' No, she doesn't have a name."

To watch *Fleabag* is to fall in love with Waller-Bridge's face. It's a wildly expressive instrument, her eyes constantly searching as inappropriate words come out of her mouth. Sonnets could be written about the way her eyebrows move when she's messing with someone. You can't help but focus on her birthmark just below her hairline, or the ideal shade of red lipstick that surrounds her teeth. Fleabag is often an insufferable character, someone who deliberately sabotages each of her relationships. And yet, thanks to Waller-Bridge, you are desperate to spend time in her filthy, funny company.

Although her current rise feels meteoric, Phoebe Waller-Bridge took a while to become Phoebe Waller-Bridge. Right out of drama school, she was Phoebe Waller-Bridge, Struggling Actress, who couldn't get a part. The story of Waller-Bridge's ascent involves the art of making people comfortable being uncomfortable. She started writing her own material along with her friend, the director Vicky Jones, and they formed the theater company DryWrite. *Fleabag* was the culmination of their efforts, starting as a play at the Edinburgh Fringe Festival in 2013.

Fleabag, in any form, is an act of confrontation, and it's what makes Waller-Bridge herself feel so simultaneously terrifying and sexy. That combination runs through almost everything she produces. It's there in the awkward humor of *Crashing*, her first TV show which dropped shortly before *Fleabag* did in the U.K. She plays Lulu, a woman who disrupts the lives of a motley crew of people squatting in an abandoned hospital when she arrives to visit her longtime best friend with whom she also has undeniable sexual chemistry. (He's engaged.) Lulu is simultaneously desperate and fully in possession of her own ability to manipulate. After *Fleabag*, she gave us *Killing Eve*. Waller-Bridge does not appear in the spy vs. assassin thriller, but she wrote it and her wild, discordant, endlessly fascinating aesthetic is infused into its very soul. Women in *Killing Eve* are fabulously dressed, horny, and often scary. It's aspirational. Who wouldn't long for Villanelle's wardrobe or just a hint of her psychopathic charm?

Waller-Bridge seems to have the ability to storm any space and make it her own, be that the Emmys or James Bond. When Daniel Craig asked her to do punch-ups on the new Bond film

No Time to Die, it seemed shocking at first. Why is this feminist writer taking on a property better known for putting women in bikinis and killing them off than treating them as full objects? But then it made perfect sense. Who better to bring the off-putting chauvinism of Bond into the modern era than someone who has a clear and wonderful disregard for prudish mores? She's a person who cites notoriously misogynistic writer Bret Easton Ellis as an inspiration because, "It makes me want to retaliate artistically," she told the *New York Times*.

Bond is just the latest cultural property she's put her stamp on: She unfathomably made a robot in a lackluster *Star Wars* film, *Solo*, cheeky and subversive. And, in the second season of *Fleabag* she injected herself into the most staid and troubled of institutions: the Catholic Church. Yes, it's impossible to discuss Waller-Bridge's impact without discussing the impact of the Hot Priest. Waller-Bridge did not want to make a second season of the show, but when the cries for more of the character got louder and louder, she got an idea. What if her heathen heroine found God in the form of an attractive man of the cloth? Andrew Scott—a supporting player in many tales of internet obsession—played "The Priest" as a male match for Fleabag, who has funneled his existential sorrow into believing in a higher power. She breaks him down as he breaks her down, and we all break down.

Waller-Bridge miraculously seems both untouchable and incredibly down to earth. When *Vogue* profiles her, she takes the reporter to a shitty bar in Midtown Manhattan where she talks about her days of snogging boys and drinking cosmos. And, yet, at the same time to acknowledge Phoebe Waller-Bridge is to acknowledge that there are geniuses walking among us. She's the type of celebrity many imagine they could be friends with if given a chance, and then become immediately paralyzed with fear. What if I meet her and I'm not clever enough? How could I possibly be up to her level?

The thing is: No one can match Phoebe Waller-Bridge. She's something of a deity herself but not any Judeo-Christian figure. Instead she's more Greco-Roman—a hedonistic agent of chaos brought into our lives to make us lust and ponder. She sends our public into a veritable panic of passion, and then she sits back, looking down on her work, taking a puff of smoke.

OTHER INTERNET GIRLFRIENDS

There's no way we could not shout out some of our other favorite Internet Girlfriends.

ST. VINCENT: Our rock goddess girlfriend, shredding in a metallic minidress.

THE U.S. WOMEN'S NATIONAL SOCCER TEAM: Our American heroes, fighting for equal pay, sticking it to Donald Trump, and getting rowdy when they win.

LIZZO: Our queen of self-acceptance, creating positive jams that lift our souls.

GILLIAN ANDERSON: We'd let her rummage through our X-Files any day.

ZENDAYA: The main proof that Gen Z is going to be okay. A multi-talented fashion icon, who has no problem shouting down racists.

THE REST OF THE CAST OF *EUPHORIA*: Zendaya's in good company with her TV costars. Hunter Schafer, Barbie Ferreira, and Alexa Demie are the future.

CARLY RAE JEPSEN: The only pop star the internet decided needed to wield a sword and then subsequently got a sword.

RIHANNA: Beyond an Internet Girlfriend. The internet's forever icon.

GRETA GERWIG: Our relatable auteur. Director extraordinaire.

CHRISSY TEIGEN: The voice of Twitter.

CATE BLANCHETT: In place of a Dark Lord we will have a queen, Queen Cate. Also, she played Carol in *Carol*, which earns her a permanent position on any list of crushes.

SANDRA OH: Hair goals. We'd let her operate on us (as in *Grey's Anatomy*) or hunt us down (as in *Killing Eve*).

FLORENCE PUGH: A rising star who does captivating cooking videos on Instagram.

ACKNOWLEDGMENTS

I hope you liked the Boyfriends and Girlfriends, and while I would like to thank Timothée for the bagels and Keanu for the memes, there are some people in my personal life I need to shout out too. First of all, my real life (not Internet) boyfriend and partner, Bob Marshall, who read drafts, provided love, and dealt with my multiple panic attacks as I wrote. The same goes for my parents, Darlene Kaplan and Steve Zuckerman. Thank you both for exposing me to an onslaught of pop culture at a very young age. My editor, Shannon Connors Fabricant, was there for me every step of the way and always willing to let me bounce ideas off of her. The rest of the team at Running Press has made for the best possible first book experience, as well. (I also owe a lot to Sarah Sullivan, who gave Shannon my email address in the first place.)

Louisa Cannell came through with stunning illustrations that made the Boyfriends and Girlfriends look just as gorgeous as they are in real life. Jen Doll has been an amazing mentor ever since I was a wee intern, and she's responsible for putting me in touch with my wonderful agent Christopher Hermelin. The entertainment team at Thrillist was supportive every step of the way. John Sellers, Leanne Butkovic, Emma Stefansky, and Dan Jackson—you are the best. A number of other friends and family were there for me during this process: Cathy Kaplan, Lindsay Gellman, Eliza Brooke, David Sims, Hillary Busis, Lauren Le Vine, Vivian Yee, and Chidi Akusobi.

I'm far from the first person to write about Internet Boyfriends or celebrity crushes and I'm forever indebted to the writers and thinkers who came before me, all of whom are referenced in the Notes section.

NOTES

INTRODUCTION

p. 1: early days of Hollywood: Those Glorious Fan Magazines | VQR Online, https://www.vqronline.org/criticism/those-glorious-fan-magazines, accessed 2 May 2020; Pamela Hutchinson, "Photoplay Magazine: The Birth of Celebrity Culture," *The Guardian*, 26 Jan. 2016, https://www.theguardian.com/film/filmblog/2016/jan/26/photoplay-magazine-hollywood-film-studios-stars-celebrity-culture.

p. 3: Sulagna Misra defined these men as such: Sulagna Misra, "How the Internet Picks Its Boyfriends," *The Cut*, https://www.thecut.com/2016/01/oscar-isaac-internet-boyfriend.html, accessed 2 May 2020.

p. 3: In *Cosmopolitan* in 2018: Emily Tannenbaum, "Internet Boyfriends Vs. Internet Husbands: Where Your Famous Bae Fits In," *Cosmopolitan*, 29 Nov. 2018, https://www.cosmopolitan.com/entertainment/a25346889/internet-boyfriend-husband-definitiion/.

p. 4: The dearly departed website *The Toast: Series If X Were Your Y, The Toast*, https://the-toast.net/series/if-x-were-your-y/page/4/, accessed 2 May 2020.

p. 5: *The Cut* meanwhile has a series: "Totally Kind Of Hot." *The Cut*, https://www.thecut.com/tags/totally-kind-of-hot/, accessed 2 May 2020.

GLOSSARY

p. 6: was coopted by just about everyone: James Hamblin, "The Death of Bae," *The Atlantic*, 30 Dec. 2014, https://www.theatlantic.com/entertainment/archive/2014/12/the-lamentable-death-of-bae/384086/.

p. 6: Big dick energy: Kyrell Grant, "'It Sucks, Because I Made Zero Dollars from It': How I Coined Big Dick Energy," *The Guardian*, 21 Dec. 2018, https://www.theguardian.com/culture/2018/dec/21/people-of-2018-big-dick-energy-buzz-phrase.

p. 6: Sometimes people who are deemed "daddy": Caitlin Dewey, "What Is the 'Daddy' Meme, and Why Are Actual Adults Fighting about It?" *Washington Post*, https://www.washingtonpost.com/news/the-intersect/wp/2016/08/22/what-is-the-daddy-meme-and-why-are-actual-adults-fighting-about-it/, accessed 2 May 2020.

p. 7: Technically, a meme, according to Merriam-Webster: *Merriam-Webster*, "meme," https://www.merriam-webster.com/dictionary/meme, accessed 2 May 2020.

p. 8: BuzzFeed once described him: Lauren Strapagiel, "Here's Everything You Need To Know About The History And Rise Of The 'Softboy,'" *BuzzFeed News*, https://www.buzzfeednews.com/article/laurenstrapagiel/heres-everything-you-need-to-know-about-the-history-and, accessed 2 May 2020.

p. 8: in a trend noticed by The Cut's Gabriella Paiella: Gabriella Paiella, "Why Does Everyone Want Their Crushes to Run Them Over?" *The Cut*, 10 Jan. 2019, https://www.thecut.com/2019/01/people-tweeting-run-me-over-at-celebrities.html.

p. 9: that can be thirsty too: Carina Chocano, "It's Easy to Be Called 'Thirsty' on Social Media. What About on Capitol Hill?" *The New York Times*, 4 Apr. 2017, https://www.nytimes.com/2017/04/04/magazine/its-easy-to-be-called-thirsty-on-social-media-what-about-on-capitol-hill.html.

p. 9: Clover Hope wrote in Jezebel that: Clover Hope, "A List of Zaddys," *Jezebel*, https://jezebel.com/a-list-of-zaddys-1796062207, accessed 2 May 2020.

MAHERSHALA ALI

p. 17: what is essentially a "formal beanie": Rachel Tashjian, "The Story Behind Mahershala Ali's

Incredible Oscars Hat," *GQ*, https://www.gq.com/story/mahershala-ali-oscars-hat, accessed 3 May 2020.

p. 18: The women of the Thirst Aid Kit podcast say he: *Mahershala, In Yellow from Thirst Aid Kit*, https://www.stitcher.com/s?eid=52646266, accessed 3 May 2020.

p. 18: all rendered in the primary tone: Lauren Larson, "Moonlight's Mahershala Ali Picks His Own Oscar Winners," *GQ*, https://www.gq.com/story/mahershala-ali-picks-his-own-oscar-winners, accessed 3 May 2020.

p. 18: His cover story very well broke the internet: Carvell Wallace, "Mahershala Ali Thinks We Can Still Make This Country Great," *GQ*, https://www.gq.com/story/mahershala-ali-moonlight-and-america, accessed 3 May 2020.

p. 18: Bossip says it all really: "The Thirst: Mahershala Ali Hasn't Left A Single Dry Panty On Twitter All Damn Day," *Bossip*, 20 June 2017, https://bossip.com/1566250/the-thirst-mahershala-ali-hasnt-left-a-single-dry-panty-on-twitter-all-damn-day/.

p. 18: Black Girl Nerds tweeted: "Going to look at more Mahershala Ali," Twitter, https://twitter.com/blackgirlnerds/status/876800527945920512, accessed 3 May 2020.

p. 18: *Harper's Bazaar* declared his smile: Erica Gonzales, "Mahershala Ali Is Living His Best Life on His New Magazine Cover," *Harper's Bazaar*, 19 June 2017, https://www.harpersbazaar.com/celebrity/latest/a10044411/mahershala-ali-gq-cover/.

p. 20: he was even passing on roles that were divine: Sanjiv Bhattacharya, "Bright Future: Mahershala Ali Is Going Places," *Esquire*, 24 Feb. 2019, https://www.esquire.com/uk/culture/film/a26445996/bright-future-mahershala-ali-is-going-places/.

p. 20: He partnered with Zegna: Cam Wolf, "Zegna and Mahershala Ali Want to Talk About Masculinity," *GQ*, https://www.gq.com/story/zegna-mahersala-ali-masculinity-campaign, accessed 7 May 2020.

TIMOTHÉE CHALAMET

p. 25: journalist Kyle Buchanan explored: Kyle Buchanan, "Call Me by Your Name's Timothée Chalamet Is a Superfan Who Made It Big," *Vulture*, 29 Nov. 2017, https://www.vulture.com/2017/11/who-is-call-me-by-your-name-actor-timothe-chalamet.html.

p. 25: and the Safdie brothers: Timothée Chalamet, "Timothée Chalamet on Why the Safdie Brothers Are His Favorite Party Crashers," *Variety*, 1 Oct. 2019, https://variety.com/2019/film/news/timothee-chalamet-josh-benny-safdie-brothers-1203353824/.

p. 25: He loves Greta Gerwig so much: "Bong Joon Ho - Martin Scorsese, Greta Gerwig and More Directors Reveal Their Onscreen Muses," *The Hollywood Reporter*, https://www.hollywoodreporter.com/lists/martin-scorsese-greta-gerwig-more-directors-reveal-onscreen-muses-1254312/item/onscreen-muses-bong-joon-ho-1254317, accessed 3 May 2020.

p. 25: The comedian Chloe Fineman does an impression: "Chloe Fineman on Instagram: 'TIMOTHEE CHALAMET Work in Prog ... @tchalamet,'" Instagram, https://www.instagram.com/p/BucKCTqnsEa/, accessed 3 May 2020.

p. 26: To be a Timmy fan: "Lil Timmy Tim - Statistics (Timothée Chalamet)," YouTube, https://www.youtube.com/watch?v=ptnvtv8VYIM, accessed 3 May 2020.

p. 26: frequent visits to Tompkins Square Bagels: Sangeeta Singh-Kurtz, "Timothée Chalamet, Benevolent Bagel King," *The Cut*, 2 Oct. 2019, https://www.thecut.com/2019/10/timothe-chalamet-shares-bagels-at-the-king-premier.html.

p. 26: named Derek, via FaceTime on another red carpet: Douglas Greenwood, "Meet Derek, the Internet's Ultimate Timothée Chalamet Stan," *I-D*, 18 Oct. 2019, https://i-d.vice.com/en_us/article/3kx458/derek-twitter-timothee-chalamet.

NOTES

NOAH CENTINEO

p. 29: in which he confessed: Allison P. Davis, "Noah Centineo, Shameless Heartthrob," *The Cut*, 14 Sept. 2018, https://www.thecut.com/2018/09/my-date-with-noah-centineo.html.

BENEDICT CUMBERBATCH

p. 33: BBC almost rejected casting him as Sherlock: Jess Denham, "BBC Doubted Casting Benedict Cumberbatch: 'You Promised Us a Sexy," *The Independent*, 28 May 2014, http://www.independent.co.uk/arts-entertainment/tv/news/bbc-doubted-casting-benedict-cumberbatch-you-promised-us-a-sexy-sherlock-not-him-9445529.html.

p. 33: "Purple Shirt of Sex," because: Keely Flaherty, "27 Times The Sherlock Fandom Won Tumblr," *BuzzFeed*, https://www.buzzfeed.com/keelyflaherty/times-the-sherlock-fandom-won-tumblr, accessed 7 May 2020.

p. 34: are 5,000 pages of content dedicated: *Sherlock (TV) - Works | Archive of Our Own*, https://archiveofourown.org/tags/Sherlock%20(TV)/works?page=5000, accessed 2 May 2020.

p. 34: as Jada Yuan noted in a profile for *New York Magazine*: Jada Yuan, "Benedict and the Cumberbitches: What Fame Looks Like From Inside a Meme," *Vulture*, 18 Nov. 2014, https://www.vulture.com/2014/11/what-fame-looks-like-for-benedict-cumberbatch.html.

p. 34: once responding to a Reddit question: "R/IAmA - I Am Benedict Cumberbatch. AMA." *Reddit*, https://www.reddit.com/r/IAmA/comments/1o8l5f/i_am_benedict_cumberbatch_ama/, accessed 2 May 2020.

p. 35: Cumberbunnies also wormed their way into the lexicon: Esther Zuckerman, "A Brief Guide to Benedict Cumberbatch Hysteria," *The Atlantic*, 18 Oct. 2013, https://www.theatlantic.com/culture/archive/2013/10/brief-guide-benedict-cumberbatch-hysteria/309811/.

RYAN GOSLING

p. 37: there was "Hey Girl" which began around 2008: "Ryan Gosling," *Know Your Meme*, https://knowyourmeme.com/memes/people/ryan-gosling, accessed 7 May 2020.

p. 37: Jezebel noted in 2009, it basically presupposes: Dodai Stewart, "Hey Girl, What If Ryan Gosling Were Your Boyfriend?" *Jezebel*, https://jezebel.com/hey-girl-what-if-ryan-gosling-were-your-boyfriend-5130274, accessed 6 May 2020.

p. 37: Danielle Henderson, a writer: Danielle Henderson, *Feminist Ryan Gosling: Feminist Theory (as Imagined) from Your Favorite Sensitive Movie Dude*, Gift edition, Running Press Adult, 2012.

p. 38: Ryan McHenry invented this format: Dan Kois, "The Creator of 'Ryan Gosling Won't Eat His Cereal' Died, and Ryan Gosling Ate Cereal in Tribute," *Slate*, May 2015, http://www.slate.com/blogs/browbeat/2015/05/04/ryan_mchenry_vine_creator_dies_and_ryan_gosling_eats_cereal_in_tribute.html.

p. 38: though he *has* said things that can be interpreted as feminist: Lauren Le Vine, "Ryan Gosling Thinks That 'Women Are Better Than Men,'" *Vanity Fair*, https://www.vanityfair.com/style/2016/06/ryan-gosling-thinks-women-are-better-than-men, accessed 3 May 2020.

p. 39: like the time he broke up a fight in New York City: "Ryan Gosling 'Embarrassed' About Breaking Up Fight," *HuffPost*, 8 Sept. 2011, https://www.huffpost.com/entry/ryan-gosling-breaking-up-street-fight_n_953802.

IDRIS ELBA

p. 41: because he just really wanted to do a musical: K. Austin Collins, "How Idris Elba Became the Coolest Man in Hollywood," *Vanity Fair*, https://www.vanityfair.com/hollywood/2019/06/idris-elba-cover-story, accessed 3 May 2020.

p. 41: playing house remixes of Lana Del Rey in Ibiza: Zach Baron, "Idris Elba Cover Story-GQ October 2013," *GQ*, https://www.gq.com/story/idris-elba-cover-interview-october-2013, accessed 3 May 2020.

p. 41: Amy Pascal said it best: Maureen Dowd, "You Have Idris Elba's Full Attention," *New York Times*, 4 Oct. 2017, https://www.nytimes.com/2017/10/04/style/idris-elba-interview.html.

p. 42: wherein he said the line that is basically the thesis: "R/DunderMifflin - Idris Elba's Reaction to Being the Sexiest Man Alive," *Reddit*, https://www.reddit.com/r/DunderMifflin/comments/9uoq5g/idris_elbas_reaction_to_being_the_sexiest_man/, accessed 3 May 2020.

p. 43: the picture practically burns a hole in your screen: Terry Carter, "Thank You Chrissy Teigen, For Baiting Idris Elba Into Sharing This Extremely Hot Photo Of Himself From 1995," *BuzzFeed*, https://www.buzzfeed.com/terrycarter/thank-you-chrissy-teigen-for-calling-out-idris-el, accessed 3 May 2020.

p. 43: a *New York Times* profile way back in 2010: Dan Kois, "A 'Wire' Star Redirects His Electricity," *New York Times*, 16 Apr. 2010, https://www.nytimes.com/2010/04/18/movies/18idris.html.

p. 44: British sitcom about a Nigerian family: Collins, "How Idris Elba Became the Coolest Man in Hollywood."

p. 44: "Yeah, I wanna be the Black James Bond": Collins, "How Idris Elba Became the Coolest Man in Hollywood."

CHRIS EVANS

p. 49: his 2011 *GQ* cover, which depicts the reporter's wild night: Edith Zimmerman, "Chris Evans Is Captain America - GQ July 2011 Cover Story," *GQ*, https://www.gq.com/story/chris-evans-gq-july-2011-cover-story, accessed 3 May 2020.

p. 49: called President Trump a racist: Zack Sharf, "Chris Evans Fires Back at Donald Trump for Being An Ego-Driven Racist," *IndieWire*, 15 July 2019, https://www.indiewire.com/2019/07/chris-evans-donald-trump-racist-tweet-1202158063/.

p. 49: declared a Straight Pride Parade in Boston homophobic: Zack Sharf, "Chris Evans Calls Out Homophobic Men Trying to Throw Boston Straight Pride Parade," *IndieWire*, 5 June 2019, https://www.indiewire.com/2019/06/chris-evans-homophobic-men-boston-straight-pride-parade-1202147699/.

p. 49: started a website: Luke Darby, "Chris Evans Is Getting Into Politics, But Probably Not the Way You Think," *GQ*, https://www.gq.com/story/chris-evans-starting-point-politics-video, accessed 3 May 2020.

p. 49: he discussed his efforts to be a good ally: Reggie Ugwu, "Chris Evans, a.k.a. Captain America, Comes Back Down to Earth," *New York Times*, 22 Mar. 2018, https://www.nytimes.com/2018/03/22/theater/chris-evans-lobby-hero-captain-america.html.

p. 50: even called in to the podcast Thirst Aid Kit: *Chris Evans (Feat. Chris Evans) from Thirst Aid Kit*, https://www.stitcher.com/s?eid=52849612, accessed 3 May 2020.

p. 50: with derpy images of pups: Nicole Gallucci, "This Wholesome Twitter Account Compares Chris Evans to Soft, Fluffy Golden Retrievers," *Mashable*, https://mashable.com/article/chris-evans-as-golden-retrievers-twitter-account/, accessed 3 May 2020.

p. 50: obsession with a singing lion toy: Syd Robinson, "14 Tweets That Prove Chris Evans' Dog Is A Very Good Dog," *BuzzFeed*, https://www.buzzfeed.com/sydrobinson1/chris-evans-dog, accessed 3 May 2020.

HENRY GOLDING

p. 57: next job was as a travel presenter for the BBC: Michelle Lhooq, "Henry Golding Is Hollywood's Next Leading Man," *GQ*, https://www.gq.com/story/henry-golding-men-of-the-year-2018, accessed 3 May 2020.

p. 57: Golding was just a total natural: Rebecca Ford and Rebecca Sun, "The Stakes Are High for 'Crazy Rich Asians' — And That's the Point," *Hollywood Reporter*, https://www.hollywoodreporter.com/features/crazy-rich-asians-how-asian-rom-happened-netflix-1130965, accessed 3 May 2020.

p. 57: handled that just about as well as he could: Alexa Valiente, "'Crazy Rich Asians' Star Henry Golding on Controversy behind His Casting in the Film: 'I'm Asian through and Through,'" *ABC News*, https://abcnews.go.com/Entertainment/crazy-rich-asians-star-henry-golding-controversy-casting/story?id=56778243, accessed 3 May 2020.

p. 58: Refinery29 even asked at some point: Anne Cohen, *Is Nick Young From "Crazy Rich Asians" A Bad Boyfriend? An Investigation*, https://www.refinery29.com/en-us/2018/08/207004/crazy-rich-asians-nick-young-henry-golding-bad-boyfriend, accessed 3 May 2020.

p. 58: he was thoughtful and charming: Lhooq, "Henry Golding Is Hollywood's Next Leading Man."

p. 59: constantly in some beautiful locale: Dana Rose Falcone, "Last Christmas Star Henry Golding Shares How He First Knew Wife Liv Lo Was 'the Love of My Life,'" *People*, https://people.com/movies/henry-golding-how-he-knew-wife-liv-lo-was-love-my-life/, accessed 23 May 2020.

p. 59: knows that it's just good sense: "Henry Golding on Instagram: 'Sometimes I Ask for Photos with Doggos Who Wear Little Roll Neck Jumpers,'" Instagram, https://www.instagram.com/p/B2cS4mSh4iJ/, accessed 3 May 2020.

JAKE GYLLENHAAL

p. 64: singing about art, can melt your heart: "Jake Gyllenhaal - Sunday in the Park with George." YouTube, https://www.youtube.com/watch?v=EuITxZnzRrw, accessed 3 May 2020.

p. 64: Gyllenhaal deadpanned: "Jake Gyllenhaal Hilariously Correct's Dan Gilroy's 'Melancholy' Pronunciation | Sundance," YouTube, https://www.youtube.com/watch?v=gre7qsGLFPU, accessed 3 May 2020.

p. 65: ballistic about Sean Paul: "'You HATE GOT?!': Tom Holland and Jake Gyllenhaal Unpopular Opinion," YouTube, https://www.youtube.com/watch?v=H3FcCz2y2mM, accessed 17 May 2020.

p. 65: He follows her: Evan Ross Katz, "Is @ms.Flufflestiltskin Jake Gyllenhaal's Cat? An Investigation," *Garage*, 23 May 2019, https://garage.vice.com/en_us/article/evyb7m/jake-gyllenhaal-cat.

OSCAR ISAAC

p. 68: that Isaac wrote himself: Wilson Morales, "Oscar Isaac Talks about Writing and Singing 'Never Had' from '10 Years'," *Blackfilm - Black Movies, Television, and Theatre News*, 14 Dec. 2012, https://www.blackfilm.com/read/2012/12/oscar-isaac-writing-singing-never-had-10-years/.

p. 68: performing a tune from his band NightLab: "Not Changing Pops Seeking," YouTube, https://www.youtube.com/watch?v=P6J14bPxiSo, accessed 2 May 2020.

p. 69: He's said he doesn't agree with her politics: Brian Hiatt, "Oscar Isaac: The Internet's Boyfriend Becomes a Leading Man," *Rolling Stone*, 18 May 2016, https://www.rollingstone.com/culture/culture-news/oscar-isaac-the-internets-boyfriend-becomes-a-leading-man-204043/.

p. 70: he eventually did: Hiatt, "Oscar Isaac: The Internet's Boyfriend Becomes a Leading Man."

p. 70: he has no Russian ancestry: Tom Shone, "Oscar Isaac on Star Wars, Guatemala and His Dylan-Esque Backstories," *Guardian*, 20 Apr. 2017, https://www.theguardian.com/film/2017/apr/20/oscar-isaac-on-star-wars-guatemala-and-his-dylan-esque-backstories.

p. 70: sometimes dealt with dead bodies: Larry Fitzmaurice, "Before Acting, Oscar Isaac's Job Was Transporting Dead Bodies," *Vice*, 23 Feb. 2018, https://www.vice.com/en_us/article/zmww8y/before-acting-oscar-isaacs-job-was-transporting-dead-bodies.

p. 71: On the *Tonight Show* Isaac explained: "Oscar Isaac's Uncle Scored a Role in Star Wars VII Using T-Shirts," YouTube, https://www.youtube.com/watch?v=UKFktbl2SjQ, accessed 2 May 2020.

p. 72: posted an Instagram of Isaac, in a bathroom: "John Boyega on Instagram: 'I Promise You All That I Won't Post Any Singing Videos at This Time but I Hope This Video Is Okay?'" Instagram, https://www.instagram.com/p/B-CUfb5pcrS/, accessed 2 May 2020.

p. 72: Carrie Fisher before her untimely death: Melissa Leon, "Oscar Isaac on the 'Pain' of Losing Carrie Fisher and Anti-Latino Hysteria," *Daily Beast*, 20 Nov. 2018, https://www.thedailybeast.com/oscar-isaac-on-the-pain-of-losing-carrie-fisher-and-anti-latino-hysteria-in-the-age-of-trump.

p. 72: bit his pal Pedro Pascal's ear on Instagram: "Pedro Pascal's Instagram Photo: 'Oscar Takes a Bite,'" Instagram, https://www.instagram.com/p/qm4Njhnw4n/, accessed 2 May 2020.

OTHER *STAR WARS* BOYFRIENDS

p. 73: *Time* magazine wrote in 2017: Raisa Bruner, "The Internet Is Swooning Over Photos of Young Harrison Ford," *Time*, https://time.com/4858421/young-harrison-ford/, accessed 3 May 2020.

p. 74: He used to eat an entire chicken: Michael Schulman, "Adam Driver, the Original Man," *New Yorker*, https://www.newyorker.com/magazine/2019/10/28/adam-driver-the-original-man, accessed 3 May 2020.

DWAYNE "THE ROCK" JOHNSON

p. 78: entire *GQ* profile of him was framed around the notion: Caity Weaver, "Dwayne Johnson for President!" *GQ*, https://www.gq.com/story/dwayne-johnson-for-president-cover, accessed 3 May 2020.

p. 78: supposedly upbeat persona Rocky Maivia: Lisa Capretto, "Dwayne Johnson Describes The Exact Moment 'The Rock' Was Born," *HuffPost*, 29 Mar. 2016, https://www.huffpost.com/entry/dwayne-johnson-the-rock-born_n_56f9844ae4b0143a9b48d978.

p. 79: sang about during one of his *Saturday Night Live* monologues: "Dwayne Johnson's Franchise Viagra Monologue - SNL," YouTube, https://www.youtube.com/watch?v=g-ciCQuUN0I, accessed 3 May 2020.

p. 79: she produces all of his films: Colleen Leahey McKeegan, "Meet the Woman Who Built Dwayne 'The Rock' Johnson's Media Empire," *Marie Claire*, 24 May 2017, https://www.marieclaire.com/celebrity/news/a27193/dany-garcia-dwayne-johnson-interview/.

p. 79: with proceeds going to Make-A-Wish: "@therock on Instagram: 'You're Gonna LOVE My New Naughty (and Nice) Ice Cream! *LINK IN BIO #Repost @saltandstraw ⋯ Jingle Bell ROCK Our Dwanta Claus…,'" Instagram, https://www.instagram.com/p/B6JOVOcFtnj/, accessed 3 May 2020.

p. 79: help military families in need: "@therock on Instagram: 'Just Stopping in to Say on Behalf of @projectrock and @underarmour We Thank You All for Your Support Our of Latest Veterans Day Apparel…,'" Instagram, https://www.instagram.com/p/B5scjPSFdCj/, accessed 3 May 2020.

p. 79: committed to women's pleasure: "Dwayne Johnson Responds to DJ Khaled's Controversial Oral Sex Comments | NME," *NME Music News, Reviews, Videos, Galleries, Tickets and Blogs | NME.COM*, 7 May 2018, https://www.nme.com/news/music/dwayne-johnson-responds-dj-khaleds-controversial-oral-sex-comments-2309835.

p. 80: party who was ostensibly in the right: Andrea Tuccillo, "Dwayne 'The Rock' Johnson Explains What Sparked Vin Diesel Feud." *ABC News*, https://goodmorningamerica.com/culture/story/dwayne-rock-johnson-explains-sparked-vin-diesel-feud-54242825, accessed 3 May 2020.

p. 80: conservative sympathies by calling young people "snowflakes": Camille Nzengung, "Dwayne 'The Rock' Johnson Stirs Controversy Over 'Snowflake Generation' Comments," *InStyle*, https://www.instyle.com/news/dwayne-rock-johnson-snowflake-generation-comments-debate, accessed 3 May 2020.

p. 80: preeminent *Ballers* fans in the country: Nicole Gallucci, "Elizabeth Warren and Dwayne 'The Rock' Johnson Had a Cute Conversation about 'Ballers,'" *Mashable*, https://mashable.com/article/elizabeth-warren-dwayne-the-rock-johnson-ballers/, accessed 3 May 2020.

p. 80: two pounds of cod a day: Walt Hickey, "Here's What Happened When Some Dude Ate Like The Rock For A Month," *FiveThirtyEight*, 4 Mar. 2016, https://fivethirtyeight.com/features/the-rock-dwayne-johnson-diet/.

MICHAEL B. JORDAN

p. 82: a life-size cutout of Jordan: Jenna Amatulli, "Innovative Teen Takes Michael B. Jordan Cardboard Cutout As Prom Date," *HuffPost*, 17 Apr. 2018, https://www.huffpost.com/entry/teen-prom-michael-b-jordan-cardboard-cutout_n_5ad63e8ae4b0edca2cbe97f2.

p. 82: Jordan invited her to the set of *Creed II*: Jenna Amatulli, "Michael B. Jordan Surprises Teen Who Brought Cardboard Cutout Of Him To Prom," *HuffPost*, 16 Aug. 2018, https://www.huffpost.com/entry/michael-b-jordan-surprises-teen-who-brought-cardboard-cutout-of-him-to-pro m_n_5b757f9ee4b0df9b093ce534.

p. 82: alongside Jordan with the caption: "I Met This Guy on Holiday," *Know Your Meme*, https://knowyourmeme.com/memes/i-met-this-guy-on-holiday, accessed 3 May 2020.

p. 83: Speaking to *GQ* back in 2018: Allison P. Davis, "Michael B. Jordan Will Be King," *GQ*, https://www.gq.com/story/michael-b-jordan-men-of-the-year-2018, accessed 3 May 2020.

p. 84: Outlier Society have inclusion riders: Mitchell S. Jackson, "When Michael B. Jordan Promises to Come Home, He Means It," *Esquire*, 20 Nov. 2019, https://www.esquire.com/entertainment/movies/a29813481/michael-b-jordan-just-mercy-interview-newark-arts-high-school/.

p. 84: homage to *Naruto*: Keenan Higgins, *Michael B. Jordan's Anime Dreams Come True With "Naruto" Coach Collab*, 5 Oct. 2019, https://thesource.com/2019/10/04/coach-michael-b-jordan-naruto-collection/.

p. 84: "I've definitely cried little man tears over anime before": Joelle Monique, "Michael B. Jordan Talks 'gen:LOCK' and His Love of Anime: 'I've Cried Little Man Tears,'" *Hollywood Reporter*, https://www.hollywoodreporter.com/news/michael-b-jordan-talks-genlock-his-love-anime-1217889, accessed 3 May 2020.

p. 85: elaborate gag for social media: "Michael B. Jordan on Instagram: 'And I'm Still KING,'" Instagram, https://www.instagram.com/p/BsUoyd5Ai6R/, accessed 3 May 2020.

p. 85: lives with his parents: Morgan Murrell, "31 Things You Probably Never Knew About Michael B. Jordan Until Now," *BuzzFeed*, https://www.buzzfeed.com/morganmurrell/michael-b-jordan-facts-photo-appreciation, accessed 3 May 2020.

p. 85: advocates for lupus research: "Michael B. Jordan on Instagram: 'My Mama about to Make Me Have to Fight Somebody She Looking so Pretty. #Oscars2019 #PopsIGotYou #DateNight,'" Instagram, https://www.instagram.com/p/BuSM9mMAyTC/, accessed 3 May 2020; Angelique Jackson, "Michael B. Jordan Supports Lupus Patients at MBJAM, Teases Return as Killmonger," *Variety*, 30 July 2019, https://variety.com/2019/scene/news/michael-b-jordan-black-panther-lupus-1203282533/.

DIEGO LUNA

p. 87: supercut of Diego Luna wanting to touch Jabba the Hutt: "diego luna really wants to touch jabba the hutt," YouTube, https://www.youtube.com/watch?v=HDU3PojzaHk, accessed 17 May 2020.

p. 89: write blog posts and TV shows: *Obsessions: We'll Always Have "Havana Nights,"* http://www.cnn.com/2011/SHOWBIZ/Movies/08/11/obsessions.dirty.dancing.remake/index.html, accessed 3 May 2020.

p. 90: Tumblr user wrote a long post: Jerico Mandybur, "Diego Luna Got Really Emotional over This Fans Touching Star Wars Post about Diversity," *Mashable*, https://mashable.com/2017/01/04/diego-luna-tumblr-story-representation/, accessed 3 May 2020.

p. 90: left Los Angeles and returned to his home in Mexico: Kate Linthicum, "Actor Diego Luna Was a Hollywood Golden Boy. So Why Did He Go Back to Mexico?" *Los Angeles Times*, 28 Mar. 2018, https://www.latimes.com/world/mexico-americas/la-fg-mexico-diego-luna-20180328-story.html.

p. 90: aimed at combating racism and poverty: Carlos Aguilar, "Diego Luna's 'El Día Después' Encourages Mexicans to Fight Racism, Classism & Corruption Post-Election," *Remezcla*, 3 July 2018, https://remezcla.com/film/diego-luna-dia-despues-gael-garcia-bernal-alfonso-cuaron/.

p. 90: though he dismisses that idea: Lulu Garcia-Navarro, "Actor Diego Luna On The 'Awakening' Around Mexico's Presidential Election," *NPR*, https://www.npr.org/2018/06/24/622567286/actor-diego-luna-on-the-awakening-around-mexico-s-presidential-election, accessed 3 May 2020.

p. 90: potentially damaging to his career: Linthicum, "Actor Diego Luna Was a Hollywood Golden Boy. So Why Did He Go Back to Mexico?"

JASON MOMOA

p. 93: in a 2014 *Chicago Tribune* interview: Curt Wagner, "Jason Momoa Takes 'The Red Road,'" *Chicago Tribune*, https://www.chicagotribune.com/redeye/redeye-jason-momoa-takes-the-red-road-game-of-thrones-stargate-sg1-20140304-story.html, accessed 3 May 2020.

p. 95: he told *Esquire* in a recent profile: Rachel Syme, "You've Seen Jason Momoa Rip Out a Man's Tongue. Now Watch Him Cuddle This Kitten," *Esquire*, 16 Oct. 2019, https://www.esquire.com/entertainment/tv/a29329407/jason-momoa-see-apple-tv-interview-2019/.

p. 95: shamed fellow superhero Chris Pratt: "Jason Momoa on Instagram: '@prattprattpratt BRO You Know My Children and I Are Madly in Love with You and I Love Everything You Do. I'm Sorry This Was Received So...,'" Instagram, https://www.instagram.com/p/B5o3uAyg6Y3/, accessed 3 May 2020.

p. 95: Metallica merch: "Jason Momoa on Instagram: 'Today Was Good Day. It's No Surprise. You Know i Fucking Love @metallica so When @billabong Just Made This Epic Line. i Called My Boy...,'" Instagram, https://www.instagram.com/p/B5JrklHAb65/, accessed 3 May 2020.

p. 95: Slayer concert with his two kids: "Jason Momoa on Instagram: 'Going on Stage and Yelling Love with My Baby Boy and Pantera. Aka @philiphanselmo and the Illegals My Mind Was Blown FUCKIN...,'" Instagram, https://www.instagram.com/p/B5iONCfgjfh/, accessed 3 May 2020.

p. 95: costar's book so she would pay attention to him: Bethy Squires, "Jason Momoa Tore Pages Out of Amber Heard's Books," *The Cut*, 7 Dec. 2018, https://www.thecut.com/2018/12/jason-momoa-tore-pages-out-of-amber-heards-books.html.

JOHN MULANEY

p. 98: specials to reference popular Broadway musicals: "John Mulaney and Broadway Musicals Combine for July 4 Fun in Viral Twitter Game," *Observer*, 4 July 2018, https://observer.com/2018/07/john-mulaney-broadway-musicals-twitter/.

p. 98: explain pop punk: Alex Darus, "Someone Hilariously Described Pop Punk Bands as John Mulaney Quotes," *Alternative Press*, 29 Jan. 2019, https://www.altpress.com/news/john-mulaney-pop-punk-bands/.

p. 98: classical music, athletes, and more: Bethy Squires, "Let's Keep This 'Things As John Mulaney Quotes' Meme Going," *Vulture*, 31 Jan. 2019, https://www.vulture.com/2019/01/lets-keep-this-things-as-john-mulaney-quotes-meme-going.html.

p. 99: an *SNL* monologue in early 2020 he joked: "John Mulaney Monologue – SNL," YouTube, https://www.youtube.com/watch?v=jRLH8E_CpP0, accessed 3 May 2020.

p. 99: would sneak jokes into the cue cards: Sean Fitz-Gerald, "Watch Bill Hader Lose It During Hilarious Stefon Sketch on 'Saturday Night Live,'" *Thrillist*, https://www.thrillist.com/entertainment/nation/snl-watch-host-bill-hader-reprise-fan-favorite-character-stefon, accessed 3 May 2020.

p. 100: created a frenzy online: Jamie Feldman, "John Mulaney Looks Like A Snack And The Whole Internet Wants A Bite," *HuffPost*, 6 Feb. 2020, https://www.huffpost.com/entry/john-mulaney-hot-photo_n_5e3c7024c5b6b70886fc7390.

p. 101: got sober when he was twenty-three: Bruce Fretts, "The Stealth Success of John Mulaney," *New York Times*, 30 Apr. 2018, https://www.nytimes.com/2018/04/30/arts/television/john-mulaney-kid-gorgeous.html.

p. 101: adorable odd couple funny guy friendship: Joanna Robinson, "S.N.L.: The Reason John Mulaney Helped Pete Davidson Make a Triumphant Return," *Vanity Fair*, https://www.vanityfair.com/hollywood/2019/01/snl-pete-davidson-john-mulaney-sober-the-mule-weekend-update, accessed 3 May 2020.

DEV PATEL

p. 105: "The secret behind Dev Patel's luscious hair": Alexis Benveniste, "The Secret behind Dev Patel's Luscious Hair," *Page Six*, 23 Feb. 2017, https://pagesix.com/2017/02/22/the-secret-behind-dev-patels-luscious-hair/.

p. 105: "Can We Take a Moment for Dev Patel's David Copperfield Hair?": Hunter Harris, "Can We Take a Moment for Dev Patel's David Copperfield Hair?" *Vulture*, 7 Sept. 2019, https://www.vulture.com/2019/09/the-personal-history-of-david-copperfield-dev-patels-hair.html.

p. 105: "I, Too, Would Leave My Fiancé for Dev Patel": Sangeeta Singh-Kurtz, "I, Too, Would Leave My Fiancé for Dev Patel," *The Cut*, 21 Oct. 2019, https://www.thecut.com/2019/10/dev-patels-hair-dazzles-in-modern-love.html.

p. 105: mother encouraged him to audition: Kate Kellaway, "Dev Patel: 'I'm Just This Guy from Rayners Lane – How the Hell Did This Happen?'" *Guardian*, 15 Jan. 2017, https://www.theguardian.com/film/2017/jan/15/dev-patel-lion-observer-interview.

p. 106: who convinced him to cast Patel as the lead in *Slumdog Millionaire*: Lynn Hirschberg, "Dev Patel Has a Very Unusual But Very Effective Tip for Winning on Oscars Night," *W Magazine | Women's Fashion & Celebrity News*, https://www.wmagazine.com/story/dev-patel-lion-movie-interview/, accessed 3 May 2020.

p. 107: outwardly frustrated with the roles he was offered: Ben Child, "Dev Patel Attacks Hollywood over Lack of Roles for Asian Actors," *Guardian*, 11 Aug. 2010, https://www.theguardian.com/film/2010/aug/11/dev-patel-asian-roles-slumdog.

p. 108: rubs Cetaphil moisturizer into his scalp: John Horn and Kyle Buchanan, "Dev Patel on Oscar Attention, Typecasting, and Hair-Care Secrets," *Vulture*, https://www.vulture.com/2017/02/lions-dev-patel-on-his-oscar-nomination-and-typecasting.html, accessed 3 May 2020.

JOHN CHO

p. 110: hashtag #StarringJohnCho and photoshopped Cho's face: *#STARRINGJOHNCHO*, http://starringjohncho.com, accessed 3 May 2020.

p. 111: told the *New York Times*: Kathryn Shattuck, "John Cho on Heritage, Hashtags and Hollywood's Surprises," *New York Times*, 19 Apr. 2019, https://www.nytimes.com/2019/04/19/

arts/john-cho-cowboy-bebop-star-trek-twilight-zone.html.

BILLY PORTER

p. 114: that opens on cue thanks to a microcontroller: Patrick Lucas Austin, "The Tech Team Behind Billy Porter's Incredible Grammys Hat Told Us How It Works," *Time*, https://time.com/5772588/billy-porter-grammys-hat-design/, accessed 3 May 2020.

p. 115: writing it just for him: Matt Grobar, "'Pose' Star Billy Porter Discusses Being 'Set Free' By FX Series," *Deadline*, 12 Aug. 2019, https://deadline.com/video/pose-ryan-murphy-billy-porter-emmys-fx-video-panel-news/.

p. 115: refusing to play the stereotypes: Billy Porter, "Billy Porter: The First Time I Refused to Keep Playing a Stereotype," *New York Times*, 21 Nov. 2017, https://www.nytimes.com/2017/11/21/theater/billy-porter-the-first-time-i-refused-to-keep-playing-a-stereotype.html.

p. 116: "You're Not Living Your Best Life 'Til You've Heard Billy Porter's 7 Rules To Live By": Chantal Follins and Ehis Osifo, "Billy Porter From 'Pose' Gave Us 7 Rules To Live By And They're Actually Genius," *BuzzFeed*, https://www.buzzfeed.com/ehisosifo1/billy-porter-pose-life-advice-cocoa-butter, accessed 3 May 2020.

p. 116: In an interview with *Esquire*, he declared: Justin Kirkl, "Billy Porter Arrived a Long Time Ago. The World Finally Caught Up," *Esquire*, 9 June 2019, https://www.esquire.com/entertainment/tv/a27817829/billy-porter-pose-interview-2019/.

p. 116: "present for the younger generation, so I can help them": Miranda Bryant, "Pose Star Billy Porter: 'I Should Have Put This Dress on 20 Years Ago,'" *Guardian*, 15 Sept. 2019, https://www.theguardian.com/fashion/2019/sep/15/fx-pose-star-billie-porter-interview.

p. 116: "I want to flip the question of what it means to be a man": Jaime Lowe, "Billy Porter on the Tonys Red Carpet," *New York Times*, 9 June 2019, https://www.nytimes.com/2019/06/09/fashion/billy-porter-tonys-red-carpet.html.

p. 117: her mouth wide open, gazing upon his finery: Brendan Haley, *Glenn Close Gagging at Billy Porter's Oscar Dress Is All of Us*, 25 Feb. 2019, https://www.pride.com/celebrities/2019/2/25/glenn-close-gagging-billy-porters-oscar-dress-all-us.

KEANU REEVES

p. 121: "Little Keester" in an *Entertainment Weekly* interview: Melina Gerosa, "Keanu Reeves, the next Action Star?" *EW*, https://ew.com/article/1994/06/10/keanu-reeves-next-action-star/, accessed 2 May 2020.

p. 121: noting how good he was at acting dumb: Chris Willman, "The Radical Reality of Keanu Reeves," *Los Angeles Times*, 17 July 1991, https://www.latimes.com/archives/la-xpm-1991-07-17-ca-2394-story.html.

p. 121: quick detour for "Sad Keanu": "Sad Keanu," *Know Your Meme*, https://knowyourmeme.com/memes/sad-keanu, accessed 2 May 2020.

p. 123: he takes in lieu of private cars: "Keanu Reeves gave his seat to a woman in NYC Subway (down-to-earth)," YouTube, https://www.youtube.com/watch?v=6X3faCM-ZIk, accessed 2 May 2020.

p. 123: emergency landing leaves them stranded: Robert Price, "Keanu Reeves, Diverted to Bakersfield Airport, Makes the Best of It," *Bakersfield Californian*, https://www.bakersfield.com/news/keanu-reeves-diverted-to-bakersfield-airport-makes-the-best-of-it/article_c5a92510-4fdf-11e9-9557-077592ee7952.html, accessed 2 May 2020.

p. 123: imprint for avant-garde books: Max Lakin, "Keanu Reeves Is Doing a New Thing: Publishing Books," *New York Times*, 16 Aug. 2018, https://www.nytimes.com/2018/08/16/t-magazine/keanu-reeves-art-book-publishing.html.

p. 123: his longtime girlfriend: Elyse Dupre, "Keanu Reeves & Girlfriend Alexandra Grant Have Been Dating for Years," *E! Online*, 7 Feb. 2020, https://www.eonline.com/news/1120542/keanu-reeves-and-his-girlfriend-alexandra-grant-have-been-dating-for-a-lot-longer-than-you-thought.

p. 123: Stephen Colbert asks him what happens when we die: "What do you think happens when we die, Keanu Reeves?" YouTube, https://www.youtube.com/watch?v=7c2olMFEhK8, accessed 2 May 2020.

PAUL RUDD

p. 125: Billy Eichner poses a question to a passerby: "Billy on the Street with CHRIS EVANS!!! (And surprise guests!)," YouTube, https://www.youtube.com/watch?v=9Zja_cIAwY8, accessed 17 May 2020.

p. 125: Vulture's "Can You Tell Which Paul Rudd Is Older?": Jesse David Fox, "Can You Tell Which Paul Rudd Is Older? (We Doubt It)," *Vulture*, 5 Apr. 2019, https://www.vulture.com/2013/03/take-our-ageless-paul-rudd-quiz.html.

p. 126: He's been playing the same joke: Steve Greene, "Paul Rudd's Recurring Gag with Conan O'Brien Hits 15 Years," *IndieWire*, 23 Oct. 2019, https://www.indiewire.com/2019/10/paul-rudd-conan-prank-mac-and-me-clip-1202184070/.

p. 127: takes photos of fellow celebrities: "Paul Rudd Does a Historic Dab While Eating Spicy Wings | Hot Ones," Youtube, https://www.youtube.com/watch?v=gWVHses2GCY, accessed 1 June 2020.

p. 128: I once argued *against*: Joe Reid, David Sims, Esther Zuckerman, Kevin O'Keeffe, and Shirley Li, "Is 'Guardians of the Galaxy' Star Chris Pratt Hot or Funny? The Wire Investigates," *The Atlantic*, 31 July 2014, https://www.theatlantic.com/culture/archive/2014/07/is-guardians-of-the-galaxy-star-chris-pratt-hot-or-funny-the-wire-investigates/375326/.

KUMAIL NANJIANI

p. 130: first beefcake photo on Instagram: "@kumailn on Instagram: 'I Never Thought I'd Be One of Those People Who Would Post a Thirsty Shirtless, but I've Worked Way Too Hard for Way Too Long so Here We . . .,'" Instagram, https://www.instagram.com/p/B6I7b2bnuJz/, accessed 3 May 2020.

p. 132: his dad made socks with those pictures on them: Maria Pasquini, "Kumail Nanjiani's Dad Proudly Owns a Pair of Socks with the Actor's Shirtless Photo on Them," *People*, https://people.com/movies/kumail-nanjiani-dad-shirtless-photo-socks/, accessed 3 May 2020.

p. 132: cosplay his favorite movies: Brian Raftery, "Kumail Nanjiani Can Be Your Hero, Baby," *Men's Health*, 10 Mar. 2020, https://www.menshealth.com/fitness/a31195173/kumail-nanjiani-buff-interview/.

p. 132: the midst of the coronavirus crisis: Kumail Nanjiani, "Every Cent of Revenue from This Podcast Will Go to @funds4disaster, @RWCFNYC, & @FeedingAmerica Who Are Working to Support Health Care, Restaurant Workers & Hungry Children. This Is Not a Podcast about the Coronavirus. We Will Be Giving Tips on How to Avoid Cabin Fever, Giving . . .," @kumailn, 19 Mar. 2020, https://twitter.com/kumailn/status/1240677851050831872.

HARRY STYLES

p. 136: singer's first *Rolling Stone* cover story: Cameron Crowe, "Harry Styles: Singer Opens Up About Famous Flings, Honest New LP," *Rolling Stone*, 18 Apr. 2017, https://www.rollingstone.com/music/music-features/harry-styles-new-direction-119432/.

p. 137: "Cos I've met the other sort": Tom Lamont, "Harry Styles: 'I'm Not Just Sprinkling in Sexual Ambiguity to Be Interesting,'" *Guardian*, 14 Dec. 2019, https://www.theguardian.com/music/2019/dec/14/harry-styles-sexual-ambiguity-dating-normals-rocking-a-dress.

p. 137: nudity or clothes swapping is involved: Rob Sheffield, "The Eternal Sunshine of Harry

Styles," *Rolling Stone*, 26 Aug. 2019, https://www.rollingstone.com/music/music-features/harry-styles-cover-interview-album-871568/.

p. 137: "We're all a little bit gay, aren't we?": Olivia Singh, "9 Times Harry Styles Was a Champion for the LGBTQ Community," *Insider*, https://www.insider.com/harry-styles-supported-lgtbqia-community-2018-7, accessed 3 May 2020.

p. 137: "Tina, she's gay": "Harry Styles Stopped Mid-Concert To Help A Fan Come Out To Her Mom," *BuzzFeed News*, https://www.buzzfeednews.com/article/skarlan/tina-shes-gay, accessed 3 May 2020.

p. 137: his bandmates were openly uncomfortable: Miranda Popkey, "Why Do Adult Women Love One Direction Slash Fanfiction?" *Vice*, 26 Aug. 2015, https://www.vice.com/en_us/article/evg4gm/why-do-adult-women-love-one-direction-slash-fanfiction.

p. 138: a cheekiness to the look: Sheffield, "The Eternal Sunshine of Harry Styles."

p. 138: he dresses this way: Lamont, "Harry Styles: 'I'm Not Just Sprinkling in Sexual Ambiguity to Be Interesting.'"

K-POP

p. 139: around since the 1990s: Aja Romano, "How K-Pop Became a Global Phenomenon," *Vox*, 16 Feb. 2018, https://www.vox.com/culture/2018/2/16/16915672/what-is-kpop-history-explained.

p. 139: BTS was declared the biggest: Julia Hollingsworth, "How South Korean Group BTS Became the World's Biggest Boy Band," *CNN*, https://www.cnn.com/2019/06/01/asia/bts-kpop-us-intl/index.html, accessed 3 May 2020.

STANLEY TUCCI

p. 141: novelty t-shirts like the one: *I Like My Coffee Like Stanley Tucci Hot Funny Male Celeb Cool Fan T Shirt | Amazon.Com*, https://www.amazon.com/Coffee-STANLEY-TUCCI-Funny-Shirt/dp/B06WGXF6SY, accessed 3 May 2020.

p. 141: BuzzFeed posts like "Stanley Tucci Is Insanely Hot . . .": Christian Zamora, "Stanley Tucci Is Insanely Hot In 'Easy A' And We Need To Talk About It," *BuzzFeed*, https://www.buzzfeed.com/christianzamora/stanley-tucci-and-his-tight-gray-shirts, accessed 3 May 2020.

p. 141: Vulture once contributed to the Tucci love: Anne T. Donahue, "Stanley Tucci's 12 Most Adorable Movie Roles," *Vulture*, 11 Nov. 2019, https://www.vulture.com/article/stanley-tucci-best-movies.html.

p. 142: sex symbol status when he played the stern father: Gabriella Paiella, "I Simply Love Tony Shalhoub," *The Cut*, 19 June 2018, https://www.thecut.com/2018/06/tony-shalhoub-appreciation-essay.html.

p. 142: silver fox zaddy status: Yohana Desta, "Andy Garcia Is Book Club's Handsome Secret Weapon," *Vanity Fair*, https://www.vanityfair.com/hollywood/2018/05/andy-garcia-book-club-interview, accessed 3 May 2020.

p. 142: appears all muscled up in a tank top: David Hudson, "People Are Taking a Moment to Appreciate the Hotness of Stanley Tucci," *Queerty*, 6 Sept. 2019, https://www.queerty.com/people-taking-moment-appreciate-hotness-stanley-tucci-20190906.

p. 143: CNN travel show: *Stanley Tucci: Searching for Italy*: Mike Pomranz, "Stanley Tucci Will Host His Own Culinary Travel Show on CNN," *Food & Wine*, https://www.foodandwine.com/news/stanley-tucci-italian-food-series-cnn, accessed 3 May 2020.

p. 144: twenty-six-pound suckling pig together: Frank Bruni, "Hollywood Ending, With Meatballs," *New York Times*, 2 Oct. 2012, https://www.nytimes.com/2012/10/03/dining/stanley-tucci-actor-writer-family-cook.html.

NOTES

CARDI B

p. 148: 2016 tweet she explained how to pronounce: "This is how my name is pronounce," Twitter, https://twitter.com/iamcardib/status/738097395364442114, accessed 3 May 2020.

p. 148: her manager suggested she try stripping: Allison P. Davis, "Cardi B Was Made to Be This Famous," *The Cut*, 12 Nov. 2017, https://www.thecut.com/2017/11/cardi-b-was-made-to-be-this-famous.html; Rob Haskell, "Cardi B: Unfiltered, Unapologetic, Unbowed," *Vogue*, https://www.vogue.com/article/cardi-b-cover-january-2020, accessed 3 May 2020.

p. 149: perfectly summed up her appeal: Clover Hope, "America Loves Cardi B, Love & Hip-Hop's Best New Cast Member," *The Muse*, https://themuse.jezebel.com/america-loves-cardi-b-love-hip-hops-best-new-cast-me-1751169948, accessed 3 May 2020.

p. 149: a video she posted in September 2019: "Cardi B on Instagram: 'Ya Hoes Better Learn,'" Instagram, https://www.instagram.com/p/B19-Je9g0xa/, accessed 3 May 2020.

p. 150: even cosmetically: "Cardi B's Dentist Told Me It Would Cost $40k To Fix My Teeth," *BET*, https://www.bet.com/style/living/2017/10/11/i-didn-t-get-a-bag--but-i-visited-cardi-b-s-dentist-anyway.html?cid=facebook, accessed 3 May 2020.

p. 150: without makeup or washing her face on Twitter: "Ok so I woke up with last night make up on," Twitter, https://twitter.com/iamcardib/status/1209838765058985985, accessed 3 May 2020.

p. 150: battling charges stemming from a fight: "Cardi B Discussed Payment, Had Friend Shoot Video of NYC Club Fight: Court Docs," *NBC New York*, https://www.nbcnewyork.com/news/local/cardi-b-indictment-new-york-city-strip-club-fight-bartending-sisters-queens-offset/1639782/, accessed 3 May 2020.

p. 150: Greta Gerwig praised Cardi's pregnancy content: Chloe Malle, "Greta Gerwig on the Twin Adventures of Filmmaking and Motherhood," *Vogue*, https://www.vogue.com/article/greta-gerwig-cover-january-2020, accessed 3 May 2020.

p. 151: told *GQ* she's "obsessed with presidents": Caity Weaver, "Cardi B on Her Unstoppable Rise, Repping Gang Life, and the Peril of Butt Injections," *GQ*, https://www.gq.com/story/cardi-b-invasion-of-privacy-profile, accessed 3 May 2020.

p. 150: Her activist statements: Haskell, "Cardi B: Unfiltered, Unapologetic, Unbowed."

LAURA DERN

p. 154: because she wanted to make her own: Sloane Crosley, "Cover Story: Laura Dern's Big Little Truths," *Vanity Fair*, https://www.vanityfair.com/hollywood/2019/01/laura-dern-cover-story, accessed 3 May 2020.

p. 156: at an NBA game: Rebecca Rubin, "Laura Dern Thinks She Saw Baby Yoda at a Basketball Game," *Variety*, 3 Dec. 2019, https://variety.com/2019/tv/news/laura-dern-baby-yoda-1203422539/.

p. 156: Baby Yoda at NBA games her thing, sort of: "@lauradern on Instagram: 'Caught a Game to See If I Could Find Him Again. #BabyYoda,'" Instagram, https://www.instagram.com/p/B5rci2hh8qQ/, accessed 3 May 2020.

p. 156: TikTok she made dancing with her daughter: "Laura Dern Dancing to Doja Cat on TikTok Is All You Need to See Today," *The Daily Dot*, 22 Dec. 2019, https://www.dailydot.com/unclick/laura-dern-tiktok/.

p. 156: gets fried chicken: Crosley, "Cover Story: Laura Dern's Big Little Truths."

p. 156: Courteney Cox for fourteen years now: "@lauradern on Instagram: 'Christmas Eve Morning Ritual Year 14!!!! Love to All!'" Instagram, https://www.instagram.com/p/B6eIo9dBwj4/, accessed 3 May 2020.

JANELLE MONÁE

p. 160: part of Cindi Mayweather, a robot who fell in love: Jenna Wortham, "How Janelle Monáe Found Her Voice," *New York Times*, 19 Apr. 2018, https://www.nytimes.com/2018/04/19/magazine/how-janelle-monae-found-her-voice.html.

p. 160: she would say, "I only date androids": Brittany Spanos, "Janelle Monáe Frees Herself," *Rolling Stone*, 26 Apr. 2018, https://www.rollingstone.com/music/music-features/janelle-monae-frees-herself-629204/.

p. 160: Jenkins himself was surprised: Wortham, "How Janelle Monáe Found Her Voice."

p. 161: character's sexuality in the final cut of the film: Susana Polo, "Thor: Ragnarok Doesn't Have an LGBTQ Hero — but Tessa Thompson Played Her That Way," *Polygon*, 25 Oct. 2017, https://www.polygon.com/2017/10/25/16545022/thor-ragnarok-valkyrie-bisexual-tessa-thompson.

p. 162: their relationship and their social media posts: Anna Silman, "A History of Janelle Monáe And Tessa Thompson's Maybe-More-Than Friendship," *The Cut*, 26 Apr. 2018, https://www.thecut.com/2018/04/janelle-monae-pansexual-relationship-with-tessa-thompson.html.

p. 162: eventually opening up: Spanos, "Janelle Monáe Frees Herself."

p. 162: "#IAmNonBinary": "There is absolutely nothing better than living outside the gender binary," Twitter, https://twitter.com/janellemonae/status/1215782996965355521, accessed 3 May 2020.

p. 162: declaration of her own identity: Roxane Gay, "Janelle Monáe's Afrofuture," *The Cut*, 3 Feb. 2020, https://www.thecut.com/2020/02/janelle-monae-afrofuture.html.

KRISTEN STEWART

p. 166: "cult-y, weird, indulgent . . . girly" role: "Kristen Stewart Assures Fans Her 'Twilight' Romance Was Real," YouTube, https://www.youtube.com/watch?v=68BWgpj9T5k, accessed 3 May 2020.

p. 166: suffering from debilitating anxiety: Megan Friedman, "8 Things You Never Knew About Kristen Stewart," *Marie Claire*, 18 Aug. 2015, https://www.marieclaire.com/celebrity/news/a15567/kristen-stewart-marie-claire-quotes/.

p. 166: "Kristen Stewart's 7 Most Awkward 'Twilight' Interviews": Lauren Otis, "Kristen Stewart's 7 Most Awkward 'Twilight' Interviews," *Complex*, https://www.complex.com/pop-culture/2011/11/kristen-stewart-7-most-awkward-twilight-interviews/, accessed 3 May 2020.

p. 166: caught cheating: Mike Fleeman, "Kristen Stewart, Robert Pattinson, Rupert Sanders Timeline," *People*, https://people.com/celebrity/kristen-stewart-robert-pattinson-rupert-sanders-timeline/, accessed 3 May 2020.

p. 166: She told *Marie Claire*: Friedman, "8 Things You Never Knew About Kristen Stewart."

p. 167: A-S-S on her basement wall: Nicholas Haramis, "Kristen Stewart, the Good Bad Girl," *New York Times*, 17 Aug. 2016, https://www.nytimes.com/2016/08/17/t-magazine/entertainment/kristen-stewart-the-good-bad-girl.html.

p. 167: "like so gay, dude": "Kristen Stewart Monologue – SNL," YouTube, https://www.youtube.com/watch?time_continue=14&v=Qc4ahnZzVM4&feature=emb_logo, accessed 3 May 2020.

p. 167: Totino's sketch captures the intoxicatingly rebellious energy: "Totino's with Kristen Stewart – SNL," YouTube, https://www.youtube.com/watch?v=A4kpVO56OBU, accessed 3 May 2020.

p. 168: brimming with unguarded passion: "Kristen Stewart Breaks Down Her Career, from Panic Room to Twilight | Vanity Fair," YouTube, https://www.youtube.com/watch?v=LrBn0g6g0H4, accessed 3 May 2020.

p. 168: feature film about a woman coming to terms: Zack Sharf, "Kristen Stewart Plans to Direct Bisexual Drama 'The Chronology of Water,' Explains Why She Would Play A Male Character," *IndieWire*, 16 May 2018, https://www.indiewire.com/2018/05/kristen-stewart-direct-bisexual-chronology-of-water-1201965222/.

p. 168: act the part of someone who was always enthusiastic: Jessica Hundley, "Kristen Stewart: Young Blood," *Dazed*, 12 Sept. 2009, https://www.dazeddigital.com/artsandculture/article/23959/1/kristen-stewart-young-blood.

ROBERT PATTINSON

p. 169: "26 Times Robert Pattinson Was A Total Freakin' Weirdo": Mackenzie Kruvant, "26 Times Robert Pattinson Was A Total Freakin' Weirdo," *BuzzFeed*, https://www.buzzfeed.com/mackenziekruvant/robert-pattinson-is-a-beautiful-secret-weirdo, accessed 3 May 2020.

p. 169: "Robert Pattinson's Viral Moments, Ranked": Iana Murray, "Robert Pattinson's Viral Moments, Ranked," *GQ*, https://www.gq.com/story/robert-pattinson-viral-moments-ranked, accessed 3 May 2020.

p. 170: ragging on *Twilight* while at the same time promoting: "Robert Pattinson Hates Twilight," YouTube, https://www.youtube.com/watch?v=nFA6Ycch1EM, accessed 3 May 2020.

p. 170: because of his years of celebrity: "Robert Pattinson Desperately Needs a New York City Hot Dog | GQ," YouTube, https://www.youtube.com/watch?v=9kdy6IpoHEI, accessed 3 May 2020.

p. 170: For more Pattinson oddness: Ramin Setoodeh, "Robert Pattinson and Jennifer Lopez on Batman, 'Hustlers' and 'The Lighthouse,'" *Vanity Fair*, https://variety.com/2019/film/actors/jennifer-lopez-robert-pattinson-batman-hustlers-the-lighthouse-1203402753/, accessed 1 June 2020.

PHOEBE WALLER-BRIDGE

p. 173: hand she has a vodka gimlet: Lauren Collins, "The World According to Phoebe Waller-Bridge," *Vogue*, https://www.vogue.com/article/phoebe-waller-bridge-cover-december-2019, accessed 3 May 2020.

p. 174: Phoebe Waller-Bridge, Struggling Actress, who couldn't get a part: Amanda Hess, "Phoebe Waller-Bridge Will Make You Laugh So Hard It Hurts," *New York Times*, 14 Feb. 2019, https://www.nytimes.com/2019/02/14/theater/phoebe-waller-bridge-fleabag-killing-eve.html.

p. 176: Bret Easton Ellis as an inspiration: Hess, "Phoebe Waller-Bridge Will Make You Laugh So Hard It Hurts."

p. 177: snogging boys and drinking cosmos: Collins, "The World According to Phoebe Waller-Bridge."